PLANNING THE PERFECT HIT

"When you plan a job, it's not so much a murder as it is a game. It is when the planning ends that the so-called deadly game begins.

"You realize that you are about to become the most important man in the victim's life, for you are going to be the last thing he sees before he dies.

"It is mostly a wonderful feeling." —Joey

"My interview with Joey was one of the most hair-raising experiences I have had in my 32 years of broadcasting. . . . We checked him out through reliable sources and know he is authentic." —Alan Douglas,
NBC Radio

"Joey is a son-of-a-bitch, alive and a functioning member of our sick society." —Chris Borgen,
CBS-TV Crime Reporter

HIT #29
was originally published by Playboy Press.

Books by Joey with Dave Fisher

Hit #29
Killer: Autobiography of a Mafia Hit Man

Published by POCKET BOOKS

HIT #29

BASED ON THE KILLER'S OWN ACCOUNT

by JOEY

with
Dave Fisher

PUBLISHED BY POCKET BOOKS NEW YORK

HIT #29

Playboy Press edition published 1974

POCKET BOOK edition published May, 1975

L.

Standard Book Number: 671-78878-7.
Library of Congress Catalog Card Number: 73-91659.
This POCKET BOOK edition is published by arrangement
with Playboy Press. Copyright, ©, 1974, by Playboy Press.
All rights reserved. This book, or portions thereof, may not
be reproduced by any means without permission of the
original publisher: Playboy Press, 919 N. Michigan Avenue,
Chicago, Illinois 60611.
Front cover photograph by Mort Engel.

Printed in the U.S.A

CONTENTS

HIT #29

HIT #28

Hit number 28 was a public execution. It took place in a crowded, noisy Italian restaurant in Brooklyn. The restaurant was my only opportunity because the intended knew he had been placed on the bullseye and had holed himself up pretty good. His employers, and mine as well, resolved that problem by inviting him out to dinner and then telling me to make him the main course. I never actually found out what it was that he had done wrong, although I later heard a rumor that he had just been caught with his hand in the numbers take once too often.

It was what could be termed a classic kill. I walked into the restaurant about a quarter after nine and went directly into the men's room. On my way through the place I took one quick, very good look and saw where my man was sitting. Naturally enough, as anyone who has seen a lot of crime movies will tell you, he was sitting toward the rear of the place, facing the door. Of course, I was now coming from the men's room, which was on the side and in the rear. Which goes to show you how much you can depend on crime movies.

When I got into the men's room I had to wait until

one individual got out of the toilet, then I locked myself in and checked my .38. I put it back in my belt and returned to the restaurant.

He never saw me coming. I walked right up behind him and blasted him three times in the back of the head and neck, blowing parts of his brain into his veal marinara, and causing blood to run into the spaghetti sauce, ruining it completely. As usual, the loud noise of the .38 going off sent everyone diving under the tables. I'm sure a few people had both the time and opportunity to get a quick look at me, but I'm just as sure the memory of seeing my man's head sprawled in his spaghetti is going to keep them from remembering too well. Scared witnesses have a way of confusing details, and I had just created a restaurant full of scared witnesses. If the police tried to put together a composite drawing from the descriptions of this crowd, they would have ended up searching for the Loch Ness monster.

I left the restaurant by a door on the side—quickly, but I didn't run—and got into the stolen car I left parked outside. I drove five blocks and parked in a perfectly legal spot and abandoned the car. I walked over two more blocks and got on the uptown subway. By the time I picked up my own car, disposed of the gun and got home, it was nearly 2 A.M.

Hit number 28 earned me one paragraph on page 26 of the *New York Daily News* and $20,000 hard cash money. I liked the money better.

There were absolutely no recriminations. I was never picked up, never questioned, never bothered. In short, a perfect, professional job. It was, in fact, too easy, which is where my problems began.

Normally, after doing a hit, I stay away from heavyweight work for at least a couple of months. This way, if the coppers do have anything on their minds or police blotters, I give them every opportunity to find me and speak to me about it. Secondly, if you start knocking them off too quickly you tend to get careless. And mine is a profession in which anything less than perfection isn't easily tolerated. One mistake is all it takes to make you a state boarder. So, when it comes right down to it, I never should have taken job number 29.

Of all the hits I've done, number 29 was the strangest. More things went wrong with it than any I did before or after. Part of the reason was my own fault. I knew I should have waited before taking another job. But 28 had been such a breeze and 29 originally came from a man I regard as a friend. And then there were these horses that took just a few seconds more than I thought they would to get from start to finish. I wasn't in debt, but I wasn't rolling in money either, so I took the contract on number 29. Because I knew I had broken my normal pattern, a bad thing for a hired gun to do, I was super-careful, too super-careful. I saw potential problems where there weren't any, and missed some of the simple ones I should have seen. Everything combined to make number 29 the most dangerous, and the most interesting of my career. It is the textbook case of how *not* to make a hit.

SAY IT AIN'T SO, JOE

Number 29, from beginning to end, took place in New York City between the months of October and November, 1968. Obviously I wasn't there for every part of it, but I can fill in any blanks because I know how these things work. And I know people who know people, so I can keep pretty good track of what transpires when I need to. In this case, since I believed there was more involved than a simple contract, I felt I needed to. The whole thing started with a simple robbery which actually was not so simple. And, pure coincidence, it started the night I finished number 28.

Joseph "Tiger" Maresca is a pretty well-known numbers controller in the Bronx. For the uninitiated, the numbers is the biggest betting game in New York, and maybe in the nation. To play, an individual places a bet of any size, from a penny to whatever, on either a three-digit number or, in single action, on one number. If your number wins—the number is usually determined by the last three digits of the total betting handle at a local track—the payoff is 600 to 1 on a three-digit number and 8 to 1 on single action. The guys who take the bets off the people on the streets are the runners. The man in charge of the runners, that individual who collects from the collectors, is the controller.

For example, Joseph "Tiger" Maresca. He's worked the same section, first as a runner, then as controller, for maybe 20 years and everybody knows him and everybody likes him. I've known him since I was a kid just getting started in the business. I know he has a wife and some children, and I know that basically he is a pussycat. In fact, I'm told that he got the nickname "Tiger" because he's so soft, like a tall guy who's called "shorty," or a weak guy becomes "muscles." At one time he probably was pretty tough, he had to be to work himself into his very lucrative position, but at this point he depends more on the reputation of a man we will refer to as the "Fat Man" than his own dwindling muscle. This is okay though because the Fat Man, an individual who still controls most of the numbers in the Bronx and Westchester, has a substantial reputation. It is said he has planted more men in the ground than the National Forestry Service has put in trees.

In other words, it is usually not a good idea to bother one of his people.

Maresca normally finishes his day's work on 139th Street and St. Ann's Avenue in the Bronx. He has a runner who lives in a building there. By the end of his day he has seen all his people and is liable to have as much as $8000 cash on him.

One night in mid-October, cash in pocket, he left his runner's apartment and started walking down the staircase. I assume he saw that there were two men standing there, waiting, but he obviously didn't think nothing about it. This was a great mistake. The two individuals—both white, one tall and the other regular-sized—were waiting especially for him. Actually there was no reason he should have noticed them.

13

They were dressed very average, and they didn't wear masks or anything silly. It's just that Maresca would have been better off if he had. The tall one pulled out a gun and pointed it right at Maresca's head. "Let's go, sweets," he said.

Maresca didn't panic, but he wasn't thrilled about the situation either. "Look," he said, "you guys go ahead and take anything you want. I ain't gonna fight yas. But don't bother me."

You really can't blame him. Normally there is very little violence connected with the numbers. There are people in this line who are violent, or have a reputation for violence, but they are usually the exceptions. Most runners are normal men. They're married, they have kids. Maybe they talk funny and rough, but they are usually very easy to get along with. They don't hurt anybody. And they don't like to get hurt.

This was fine with the thieves also. "We don't want to hurt you," the tall one told him, "we just want the money." They took him down to the basement and made him lean up against the oil burner. The money was indeed all they wanted. They didn't bother his slips—his list of who bet how much on what—and they didn't even ruffle his jacket.

"We're gonna leave you now," the regular-sized one told him after his partner had pocketed the cash. "You just stay here for awhile, because if we see your head we're gonna have to shoot it off." Then they disappeared.

Maresca immediately did absolutely nothing but stand there and shake. Until this time the worst thing that had ever happened to him were a few misdemeanor pinches. He waited about 15 minutes and then, very slowly and very carefully, went back upstairs to his runner's apartment and called the office. "I been robbed," he said.

The particular bank that Maresca worked for was located in the basement of a funeral home in East Harlem. I had worked for them at one point and I will never forget how they used to lay the money out on body slabs. Just piles and piles of bills, and on occasion, a stiff would be laid out there waiting for the embalmer or cosmetician or his funeral. I don't mind killing them, but I'm not too thrilled about looking at them. The office told Maresca not to move and they sent two men over to bring him back. By the time he arrived at the bank with his slips, the Fat Man had been contacted and had come over.

They sat Maresca down, gave him a good stiff drink to calm him down, and then they started questioning him. For five hours they grilled him and regrilled him, over and over. If he was hiding anything, or lying, he would have burned out at some point during the questioning. But he didn't. It wasn't that they didn't believe him, Maresca had been with the organization over 20 years and they had never had any problems with him before, but runners as well as controllers have been known to hold themselves up. But he was really terrified and they figured he was telling the truth.

Two days later they were completely convinced when a second controller was held up. This was an Irish kid working up in the Gun Hill section, around 214th Street and Lacombe Avenue. Again, as I later found out was true in all the robberies, the kid had just seen his last runner of the day. This particular runner lived in the project up there and he took the numbers for the whole project. The Irish kid walked out of the building and toward the parking lot. Before he reached his car, two guys, the same two guys who heisted Maresca, came up to him and stuck a gun in his ribs. The Irish kid said absolutely nothing and did absolutely nothing, he didn't resist at all. "Empty your pockets, sweets," the big one commanded. "Don't give us no trouble and we ain't gonna hurt you." They took his money and his car keys. The money was a hell of a day's pay, almost $10,000. The keys were worth maybe 30 cents. They told him they were going to leave the keys under a mailbox about two blocks away. And they did.

Now the office knew something was happening, but they weren't sure it was an inside job. They figured maybe the organization was just having some bad luck. The luck got worse.

Down at the end of Tremont Avenue in Throgs Neck, there are a bunch of private homes and a boatyard. The runner worked in the yard, taking action from all the boat crews, as well as restaurants, gas stations and bait shops in the neighborhood. Normally the controller didn't even get out of his car. He showed up about 5:30 in the afternoon, honked his horn twice and waited. The runner came out, handed him an envelope, and went back inside. Normally.

This time the controller collected his envelope and started to pull out of the parking lot. Before he could get down the driveway another car cut him off. The tall guy jumped out and had a gun pointing at the controller's head before he could make a move to back up. "Step on that accelerator, sweets, and you're dead," he said. Knowing what I know now, that these were punk stick-up men and not gunsels, I personally doubt he would have pulled the trigger. Of course, I could be wrong. But the controller was not about to test him.

"I'm yours," he shrugged. He handed over what he

had, which was about $6000. The tall man reached into the car, took out the keys and heaved them across the parking lot. Then he was gone.

By this time they were screaming bloody murder in the funeral home. It was obvious the controllers were being fingered by someone on the inside who had definite information, because robbing a controller is not as easy as it sounds. First, you have to figure out who the controller is. That in itself is not terribly difficult. But then you have to find out where he is going to be, when he's got the most money on him, and when he is going to be there. This is very difficult because a good, hustling controller may make 40 or 50 stops a day, and he never stays in any one place too long. Even if you do get his schedule, you've still got to isolate him, and since the job requires the controller to be around people, that is not very simple either. But these two stick-up men were doing it, and doing it perfectly, so it was obvious they were being fed information.

The office tried everything except calling the New York City Police Department. They had the controllers change their schedules. They started using armed guards to ride shotgun. But none of that did any good. The stick-up boys were always too quick. Before the guard could raise his shotgun they were on him. These boys did a death and destruction job on the office in October and early November. It reached the point where they were hitting the same controllers two and three times, and still the office could not get a line on who these guys were or who was supplying their information. All counted, they picked up more than $100,000.

Then, unfortunately for certain parties, they got themselves picked up.

Since it was obvious that someone in the office, presumably a controller rather than a clerk or runner, was informing the dynamic duo about every change, the Fat Man and his top buttonmen took some important steps without bothering to mention them to anyone else. They went outside their own organization and hired some heavies. They started using backup cars equipped with walkie-talkies and two of the heavies. Even the controllers didn't know they were being followed. It took about a week to grab the pair.

This particular controller had changed his schedule so he finished up at Crotona Park where 174th Street and Crotona Avenue meet. Normally he made it a point to get to the park during daylight, because you never can tell who is going to be in the park after dark. All a controller needs is to get mugged and lose his day's receipts. But these were unusual circumstances so he went after dark and was very careful. He simply pulled into a bus stop, parked, and went into the park. His runner was waiting on a bench. After receiving the works the controller headed back toward his car. Our two friends were waiting for him.

"Oh, shit," he said, "not you guys again," or something near that. At that moment I bet he wished a mugger would have showed up. The stick-up men relieved him of his daily bread. Then they told him it would be far safer for him to walk in the park rather than out of it, and started for their own car.

The regular-sized one was driving. He didn't get very far. He had just put the key in the ignition when he looked up and was surprised to discover a very large gun pointing directly at his head. The tall one had made the same discovery. "Game's over gentlemen," said one of the heavyweights. He was dead right.

The stick-up boys were named Manny Sanchez and

Allie Jacobs. Manny was the short one and Allie was the tall one. Manny lived out in the ass-end of Brooklyn and Allie came from Queens. They were simply two small-time punks and nobody within anybody's organization had ever seen them or heard of them.

The heavies brought them up to the funeral home and escorted them down into the basement. From there the buttonmen took over. The conversation covered the usual subjects: world affairs, politics, the United Nations. At first Manny and Allie were reluctant to enter the discussion with their own opinions, but they were soon persuaded that the organization did indeed care about their ideas on these subjects. It's not that Manny and Allie wanted to play hero and protect their silent partner, it's just that they took one look around, saw the empty coffins, and figured they were going to have a bad case of death as soon as they told everything they knew. So they were in no particular hurry to talk.

Therefore it was up to the buttonmen to (a) convince them they would not be hurt if they told everything they knew, or (b) convince them that being dead could actually be better than being alive. The buttonmen opted for alternative b. They used some very subtle techniques. It is a well-known fact in funeral-home basements that you can hurt a guy pretty good by poking his balls with an ice pick. Pins inserted directly under the fingernails also prove very persuasive. This was demonstrated to Allie and Manny and they showed a willingness to talk. And, as soon as they stopped screaming, they did. By the time the Fat Man had been notified and gotten down there, the boys were so eager for some friendly conversation they would have told him the last time their mothers got laid if that's what he wanted to know.

"Let's have it," the Fat Man said.

"A few months ago," Allie said, "this guy came to us and asked us how would we like to make some money. We said we'd like."

"Which guy?"

"This guy. This Joe Squillante guy. And so . . ."

"Squillante!" The Fat Man couldn't believe it. Joe Squillante had started running numbers for him in the mid-1950s. He was made a controller in 1965 and there had never been a single problem with him or his customers. The Fat Man obviously found it hard to believe that Squillante was his man. That was more than biting the hand that feeds you, that was chopping it off with a fuckin' hatchet. "Bullshit," the Fat Man challenged, "Squillante got robbed himself."

"He sets hisself up so no one suspect him," Manny said in a squeaky voice. "We went over, he give us the money, that was it. He was givin' us all the info on all them other people. Joe Squillante."

"How come he told you his real name?" the Fat Man, who wasn't at all convinced he wasn't being put on, asked.

The boys shrugged their shoulders. "We was doing some things with a bartender in Bayside and . . ." Allie started to explain.

"What sorta things?"

"Hey man, you know, things. A little collecting for people, getting some bets placed for some people, a little muscle work, a gun job . . ."

"Stick-ups only," Manny said. "We never shoot nobody. Never. I never even fired the mother."

Allie looked at him sort of disgustedly. "You know what I mean," he continued, "things. So this bartender, he told us he had this guy who maybe had some work for us. We met him and he told us he was this guy Joe Squillante. That's all."

"What'd he look like?" I guess the Fat Man figured it wasn't below some fucker to use Squillante's name.

But Manny described him perfectly. "He was like regular size. five foot ten and weighed maybe hundred 'n' seventy. He gettin' a beer belly. And he got black hair which he combs to the side and it looks like maybe he going bald in front. And plus he got one scar on his face over his eye."

"That's Squillante."

Allie continued the narrative. "So we met Squillante, or whoever he is, and he tells us he's gonna finger guys for us to stick-up. He said he was taking sixty percent and we could split the other forty. It sounded good."

"Sounds shitty to me," the Fat Man said. "You guys were taking all the chances and he was getting sixty percent. How come you guys go for such a shitty deal?"

"Hey. listen, it was still lots more than we was making anywhere else," Allie said truthfully. They had ended up making about $35.000 apiece.

The Fat Man just couldn't believe it. He turned to the man who told me this story and asked, "Why the fuck would Squillante get into this shit? The guy is making five thousand a week."

Nobody had an answer. All Manny and Allie knew was that Squillante fed them good information and never cheated them on the split. The Fat Man didn't ask any more questions. Instead, he took his button-men upstairs and held a meeting. He just left the boys sitting there. I would have to guess that they spent their time praying hard. They had to figure they were dead. but they figured wrong. The Fat Man, he needed them.

He just could not believe Joe Squillante was his man. He knew Squillante, he knew the wife, he had even been to both his kids' confirmations. In the up-stairs meeting he kept talking about the fact that he trusted Squillante, and believed in the guy, and knew the guy. Then he said he just would not blitz the punks until he was sure Squillante was his man. So he went downstairs and told them that if they followed his in-structions perfectly, there was every chance they might live to become godfathers.

They listened very, very carefully.

A hit is always bad for business so the Fat Man wanted to be sure he had the right man. He told Man-ny and Allie that they were supposed to act like noth-ing had gone wrong. Like they hadn't been picked up and they hadn't given up Squillante. He told them they were going to be given the money and a couple of slips from the controller they had held up that eve-ning. They were to give this to Squillante. But they were to inform the office before every meeting they had with him. And when Squillante outlined the next job, they were to let the office know in complete detail.

In return they would be permitted to live.

The boys allowed that this was an excellent plan.

Then the office began investigating Squillante. Even though he had been there almost 20 years, nobody could claim to know him very well other than the Fat Man. They knew he was married, where he lived, and that he kept his activities almost exclusively confined to the numbers. It was also known that he was not a big liver. He didn't have no fancy house, or big car, and he didn't mess around with broads and hit the nightclubs. He had a girlfriend but she didn't require much upkeep. So, the thing that bothered everybody was, what was he doing with the money he was making? Where the hell was he putting it?

It took them a couple of days, but they got their answer: Squillante was deep into five different bookmakers. He was losing his shirt and he wasn't paying so good. The story was that he had started out by betting $500 a week. Then he graduated to $2500 weekly and he was losing. So he went for $5000. Eventually he went into the pit for over $200,000, which is a very large pit.

Out of the clear, blue sky above the guy had become a degenerate gambler. No one seemed to know why or how come, but all of a sudden he was picking up the phone and betting his lungs. And that is what started the whole thing.

Now, he was making $5000 a week, but that was nowhere near what he owed. He must have figured that the only way he could ever get even was to go into business for himself. Unfortunately, he chose the wrong business. He went to this Bayside bartender who found him two local desperadoes. Squillante offered them this semi-golden opportunity and they jumped. He was using his share of the earnings to pay off the books.

Manny and Allie did precisely what they were told, and as they said, it was Joe Squillante who met them for the payoff and Joe Squillante who gave them the details for the next stick-up job. The office decided that Squillante had to be permanently fired. Or, as it is known within the organization, burned. That's when I got the message that somebody wanted to see me.

That was the story I was told after finding out Joe Squillante was my target. It just didn't sound like the Squillante I had grown up with.

CONTACTED
AND CONTRACTED

I get contacted to do work in many different ways. This particular message came to me on a bright, cool Thursday afternoon, while I was in the midst of some real-estate speculation. At the center of my speculation was an age-old question: How long would it take a certain three-year-old to cover some prime New York State race-track real estate? I thought one animal was a particularly good investment, and I was checking my resources to see exactly how much I cared to invest. Unfortunately, I had made a number of similar investments earlier in the afternoon and my spirits were as low as my bankroll.

I finally determined to wager $100. As I finished making what would soon prove to be another one-way trip to the window, this guy I knew from my days as a numbers controller came up to me. "How you doin', Joey?" he asked.

"Fine, how you doin'?" He was doin' fine also. We exchanged amenities. I told him business was fine, which it was. At this point in my life, besides doing my hit number, I was into a bookmaking outfit—I had about 25 of my own customers—I was boot-legging cigarettes on a reasonably regular schedule, I was occasionally doing a little shylocking, and plus I was picking up little odds and ends here and there. Finally I said, "I'm earnin', nobody's gettin' hurt, everybody's happy."

He shook his head no.

"Everybody ain't happy?" I asked.

He shook his head yes. "Petey wants to see you," he said. This individual didn't know what it was about, he was just passing a message along, but he knew it meant no good for somebody.

Petey is a buttonman. He controls a certain territory for the Fat Man, which means he gets a piece of every bit of action that takes place in that area, from numbers to card games. He and I go back a long way, back to the time I came back to New York to hunt down the last of the three men who killed my first wife. During that time he helped me out by getting me a few jobs where I could earn good without too much effort.

More importantly, he is one of the very few people alive today who knows my real name and what I do for a living. He knows I'm a hit man. And he knows I do good work. Unfortunately, he also knew he could find me at the track, which is a bad habit I've gotten into. I knew if Petey wanted to see me he had some work for me. And I'm always willing to listen to propositions.

I left the track after the eighth race and stopped at a pay phone. The gist of the message was to contact him at a certain bar where he likes to hang out. When I called and asked for him I was told he wouldn't be there until 11 o'clock that night. That was nothing unusual. Petey has a girlfriend he likes to see plus he has a lot of business to supervise. I knew I'd get him then.

I had work of my own to do. I called my bookmaking office to see what my customers were doing. As with every book, a runner is responsible for servicing his own customers, so he has to keep in contact with the clerks in the office. By the time I called, the day's animal action was in and the clerks were working on it. They gave me the figures for the afternoon and we had done a little heavier than I would have guessed. The phones were already ringing for the nighttime sports and trotting action. As usual, the office wanted to check some credit lines with me.

Each bettor has a credit limit and the only person in the world who can allow him to bet more than the limit is the runner. In this case, me. First problem was this guy named Eddie who had a line of $500 and had blown $450 early in the week. He wanted to get even by going for $200 on some ball games. "No," I told them, "give him a hundred." I knew he was good for the whole $200, but lately he had become a real pain so I wanted to put him in his place. He was one of those people who, if you give him a fucking finger, he'll take your whole arm.

The second problem was Elliott. Elliott wanted some extended credit. Now, this Elliott has been with me for five years. Whatever office I'm working with, he comes along. He is very, very rich, but he is also hung-up about being cool. He is particularly easily impressed with muscle and tough talk. In his case I wouldn't be surprised if it was a sex thing. I told them he could have all the credit he wanted.

Once I finished with the office I had the entire evening to kill before speaking to Petey. The only prior business I had was meeting two new cigarette customers. I've been in and out of the cigarette business for almost 15 years. The operation is simple: By bringing cigarettes directly from Carolina to New York and selling them, you can avoid paying any state taxes. It is a very, very profitable business. All it takes is some rental trucks, drivers, a warehouse and customers.

A friend had called me a few nights earlier and said he had two individuals in cigarettes who needed a supplier. I agreed to meet them and this third party set up the meeting. We met in a midtown restaurant so I could combine my business with my real pleasure, which is eating. I sat down, perused the menu, and we started talking. Actually they started talking and I started listening. I learned a long time ago that listening is much safer than talking, especially when you don't know who you're talking to.

It turns out that their previous supplier had been busted and they were desperate for butts. They said they could probably take as many as 2000 a week, which is a sizable order. I still hadn't said a word. Finally, without ever admitting I was indeed in the business, I asked these people to tell me the names of some people they knew who could vouch for them. One guy knew people in Brooklyn, the other guy named a couple of men in Manhattan. "Okay," I said after writing down the names, "give me your driver's licenses."

They didn't like that. "You a copper?" one of them asked as the veal parmigian arrived.

"Listen, fuck," I replied in my toughest gangsterese, "you come to me, I didn't go looking for you. You want to deal with me, you give me what I ask for. No arguments. If not, so long and goodbye. Whatta I need you for?" You've got to be strong with these type people.

"Don't get hot, don't get hot," his friend tried to calm me down. I wasn't even upset, it was an act. The only thing that was bothering me was that my veal was getting cold while those guys screwed around. Finally the peacemaker handed me his license. The big mouth did the same.

"Now you know how the game is played." I wrote down their names and their addresses from the licenses and returned them. Everything looked legitimate, so I asked for their telephone numbers. "Okay," I finally told them, "I'm not saying I'm in the cigarette business or anything like that, but if I can help you out I'll get in touch with you very shortly." I didn't even want to talk price with these guys until I was sure they weren't coppers. And I couldn't really be sure of that until I checked them out. All of that would have to wait until Friday anyway, because Petey was very firmly in my mind.

The cigarette boys and I discussed food and animals for the rest of the meal. They picked up the check, which is traditional when you've asked for a meeting, and we departed.

I've never been able to understand about the so-called sixth sense, but it definitely exists. When something is about to begin, when something is about to happen, you can feel it. You know it. I knew Petey had a hit for me, somehow I was sure of it. Even though I normally don't take jobs too soon after having completed one, and figured I probably wouldn't take this one, it is considered common courtesy to speak to people who want to speak to you. Besides, I was curious. And I could use the money for my real-estate ventures, which lately I had been making with more frequency and less return than ever before. I went to call Petey.

He was waiting to hear the melodious chimes of my voice. Except for a brief hello, how are you, fine, we got right to business. "Meet me under the Williamsburg Bridge at one o'clock," he said.

"With bells on," I told him and hung up. It was obviously not going to be a social visit.

Petey is easy to recognize any time. He has a habit of keeping his right hand inside his coat pocket when he's wearing a coat, or tucked into his belt buckle or pants waist when he's not. That and the fact that there was no one else standing under the Williamsburg Bridge at one o'clock made it very easy for me to find him.

This particular spot, right at the end of Delancy Street, is a favorite meeting place because it's quiet, dark and lonely. More than one body has been dropped there for those reasons. Petey hopped into my car and we spoke nice for a few minutes. How's your old lady? Fine, how's your old lady, Petey? Fine. When we gonna have dinner together? Whenever you're not busy. We'll have dinner. Good, where do you want to go? And so on. Finally he said, "I think I have a contract for you."

A contract is simply a verbal agreement to have something done. It does not, of necessity, involve a hit. But I knew Petey wouldn't drag me out at 1 A.M. and meet me under a bridge if he wanted to talk about hauling cigarettes. I knew it involved heavyweight work. "All right," I said, "lay the story on me."

"No story, it doesn't involve my territory. Just a message. Sunday night be at the Half Moon. When you walk in the door you'll recognize somebody you know. You go up there, you talk to him, see what you want to do."

"What time do I meet him?"

"Around nine-thirty, ten o'clock. Don't eat dinner before you go, because he'll probably want to bullshit with you for awhile."

Just exactly what I needed—another free dinner!

Obviously making hits is more enticing than cigarette deals, and more lucrative, but it's not as steady. If you're going to work within organized crime, you've got to make sure you have some sort of steady income. Personally, I usually have a few small things going. Now, cigarettes are lucrative but they require a great deal of time. Even though smuggling butts is not as serious as burning somebody, the same kind of caution that leads up to pulling the trigger goes into putting a deal together. Justice is indeed blind, she'd just as soon throw you in the clink for bootlegging cigarettes as binging some punk. And it's a whole lot easier to prove. If they catch you with a truckload of cartons, your only hope is to stack the jury with chain-smokers.

So I spent a good portion of Friday checking up on the two new dudes who wanted to order from me. They proved out clean. The kid from Brooklyn had a reputation of being a good hustler who earned good, and as far as anyone knew, was honorable in his commitments. Ditto the second guy. So I set up a second meeting.

We met in a luncheonette on Second Avenue in the upper 70s. I laid it out carefully for them. I gave them the price, which depended on how large their order was. "And," I told them, "I get paid on delivery and I get paid in cash. No such things as owesies." I told them I'd let them know when I wanted their order and how soon I could deliver.

Big Mouth from Manhattan said they had done some figuring and probably would need 2400 cartons. "How do we get in touch with you?" he asked.

"You don't," I told him.

The Half Moon is a Bronx restaurant just off 187th Street east of Arthur Avenue. The food is good and the people leave you alone, which is better. Most meetings of the type I was attending are held in restaurants or public places of some sort, unless there is a specific reason why two people should not be seen together.

I had absolutely no idea who I was supposed to meet there, so I just walked in and started looking around. I didn't have to look too far. Sitting at a table by himself was a very well-known buttonman by the name of Jackie Sweetlips. The "Sweetlips" part came from the fact that he was constantly running his tongue across his lips and, when he was nervous, his tongue would dart in and out, around and around very quickly, like a snake. He had worked as a bookmaker, a banker and now a buttonman for the Fat Man. There is a rumor that he had pulled the trigger on occasion, but I never saw anything in his character to make me believe that. For a front he ran a used-car lot on Jerome Avenue, and I don't have to mention what some of his cars were used for. I took one look at him and looked no further: I knew he was the man I was supposed to see.

I was very surprised. I had known Sweetlips off and on for maybe ten years. The last few we have not been so friendly, not since I hit a man known as Bats. Bats turned out to be Jackie's best friend. They had evidently grown up together, and gone into the mob business together. I never knew exactly what Bats had done, I was just hired to do my thing and I did it. But what I didn't know then was that friend Jackie was maneuvering to get the contract canceled. In fact, he thought he had just about settled the beef when I did Bats.

So, a few weeks later, I hear a rumor that Jackie Sweetlips is telling people he is going to "ice" me. (That's when "ice" was a very popular word.) I didn't know then and I never discovered how he found out that I was the individual who did the work. That is one fact he has no reason for knowing.

The way I found out he was looking for me was that people started asking me what I had done to him, because he wouldn't tell anybody. For a long time I didn't even know the reason. It turns out Jackie had asked somebody to see me and ask me to give Bats an extra week, so Jackie could cement his reprieve. I never got the message. It wouldn't have made any difference if I had—unless it came from the man who hired me—but I really never did get it.

Jackie didn't believe that. He thought I got the message and ignored it, so he was going to "get even." This is considered highly unprofessional. Organized crime has certain rules and regulations, and "getting even" is outlawed except in very special circumstances.

It never bothered me at all. "Let him try," I said. But he never did. Never, And there he was, sitting in the Half Moon, waiting for me. I thought it was very strange, and I began to wonder why I had been asked to do the job.

Jackie looked just as surprised to see me as I was to see him. I think it is possible he might have been confused. I've gone under so many names that it's possible he never made the connection between my physical appearance and the name the person who hired me to kill Bats knew me by. Possible, not probable.

More probably, my name had been brought up at a meeting and the Fat Man okayed it. When the Fat Man says something will be done, it's Jackie's job to make sure it happens, no matter how distasteful he might personally find it. Anyway, I was only there because of Petey.

Without Petey setting this meeting up I wouldn't have even walked into the men's room with Jackie. As soon as I saw him I would have turned around and walked out. The guy doesn't like me and I don't like him, so why antagonize each other. But I trusted Petey completely. The only way I'm going to do this type of business is through somebody who knows me and knows what I do, and who I trust. And that is Petey. After all, there are lives at stake.

All this was running through my head as I walked up to Jackie's table. "Hello Jackie," I said to him just as nicely as I could. "How are you?"

"Fine," he says.

"How's the used-car business?"

"Fine," he says. So far, as you can see, this is not such a thrilling conversation. But neither of us is one-hundred-percent-positive-sure that we are talking to the right party, so there is no sense jumping into details.

"What's doin'?" I asked him.

"Not too much." He was at least putting on a good show of being friendly.

"You bookin'?"

"Yeah, a little of that. I got a piece of a numbers bank. I got some money on the street. Those people up on Jerome Avenue go through a lot of cash, you know." I would guess he probably had close to half a million, not all his own cash, on the street. Besides having his own used-car place, he was the backbone of a number of other dealers on the block. Finally he asked me if I had eaten dinner yet and I told him I hadn't. We ordered. "What brings you up to this neighborhood?" he asked as we waited.

"I come up to see a friend of a friend about a little business."

"Yeah?" he says. "S'funny, I'm here to meet a friend of a friend also."

"Whose friend are you supposed to meet?" I asked, as if I didn't know.

He hesitated just one split second. Then he was quite definitive. "Petey."

I nodded in affirmation and smiled. My tone changed. I didn't have to be friendly any more, just do business. "Okay, whattya want Jackie, what's on your mind?"

His tongue came shooting out of his mouth and smacked across his lips. "We've got some heavyweight work. Interested?"

"I'm here, ain't I?"

He nodded as if this were the most logical thing in the world. "Then I got a contract for you."

As with Petey, I didn't want any mistakes. I wanted to make sure we were talking about the same work. "What kind of contract?"

"I want somebody hit."

"You want somebody hit?" I said, emphasizing the *you.*

"No," he corrected, "the Fat Man wants him hit." I tried to catch something in his voice or his manner- isms that would tell me what he thought about me, but it just didn't seem to be there. He looked me pretty straight in the face as he talked. There didn't seem to be any personal feelings involved.

The first few times I sat in on meetings like this I felt a sort of excitement, a sort of exhilaration. No more. Now it was business. How much. How quickly. And who. The only answer that usually made any difference was the first one.

"What's the story?"

"It's one of our controllers. He's been setting up other controllers to get jammed."

I didn't understand what he meant by that. Books and movies always show hoods talking in slang words that everybody understands. It doesn't work that way. Everybody doesn't understand everything. Of course, there are certain words that everybody in the business uses, but when a contract is being discussed there is very little flashy language. It's cut and dried and laid out on the table. "Jammed?" I asked him.

"Yeah. He's been having them heisted."

Heisted I understood. "You're kidding. What kind of prick would do something like that?"

He laughed. "A stupid one." The conversation was getting more comfortable now. As much as he might have disliked me, it was obvious he liked the individual we were discussing a whole lot less.

I laughed too. "You sure about this guy?" I didn't want to go any further if this was an iffy thing. But I really wasn't overly concerned, I knew the organization would not be going ahead unless everything had been thoroughly checked out. One important factor that helps keep organized crime healthy is that so few mistakes are made. Things are checked and double-checked.

"We got the guys who were doing the heisting. They told us the whole story. Then we set up the guy and watched him take a payoff." He paused. "Yeah, we're dead sure."

This was an interesting story. "Does he know you're on to him?"

Sweetlips shook his head no. "He's sitting like a duck floating on a pond!"

At this point I had to make the decision: commit myself or take a hike. Normally I would have said thanks for the offer but so long, because I don't like to do heavyweight work too often. You get careless, like I said. But this job seemed so easy, and the money smelled so good, and there hadn't been even the slightest tremor about number 28. After considering these things, and deciding to break a personal pattern this one time, the only thing that would have made me refuse was if I thought the designated hittee was somebody I knew and liked, or somebody that I owed something to. There are few people in this business that I am close to. And if they're up to something I usually know about it. So when he said controller and I knew there was nobody I cared about working that way, I decided to take the job. All this went through my mind before I asked the one question that binds me to the job. "Sounds alright. Who's the guy?"

"Joseph Squillante."

I started laughing.

"You know him?" Jackie asked.

"Know him shit," I said. "Raised in the same neighborhood."

Jackie's tongue came darting out of his mouth again. Friendships have been known to cause complications. It was, after all, a friendship that caused him to start hating me. "You got any qualms?"

Jackie had nothing to worry about. "He don't mean nothing to me. I've known him all my life but I don't think I've ever been inside his house. If I've had three cups of coffee with him in our lifetime that's a lot."

Actually I knew him a little better than that, but I didn't see any reason to go into it. Joe Squillante and I were raised on the same block in the East Bronx. We lived about half a block, five buildings, away from each other. Because we were about the same age we played stickball, we played softball, we played ringolevio. We would even go down to the corner with a bunch of other kids and steal food and fruit together. But it was always with other kids. We weren't close at all.

I stopped to think about Squillante. I could not understand how he had gotten himself in this situation. He was never what I would call a ballsy type of guy, much more of a follower than a leader. When I became a controller at the age of 15 he was just starting to move his ass running numbers for somebody. I never kept track of him. I mean, I would never go out of my way to ask somebody, "Hey, what's Joe Squillante up to?" but his name would pop up in conversation now and then. So I kept track of him in the sense that I would hear about him or I would run into him periodically and we would catch up with each other.

I had nothing against the guy. And I was surprised that he turned out to be somewhat of a success. A guy who works at this business can do alright. They go out, they work, they earn. That's what he did. I knew he was no dummy. I believe he graduated from James Monroe High School and then went on and had one year at City College. I knew his parents to see them, but I didn't know them to go into their home. I even met the girl he married.

I didn't go to the wedding, although I heard about it, and one day my wife and I were out shopping and there he is with his new wife, Cindy. She came from the Fordham section of the Bronx. Actually, she was pretty attractive which didn't surprise me, because Squillante was a decent looking guy. He was about 5'9" tall and 165 pounds. He had long, wavy black hair like most Italian singers do. After they were married they lived in the neighborhood for awhile and then they moved up to Fordham. They stayed there awhile and, after Cindy had a few kids, they moved over to Pelham Bay.

Jackie didn't say anything while I was thinking. "Listen, you got any bad feelings, that's okay. We'll just get somebody else."

"I ain't got no bad feelings, Jackie. I know the guy, that's all." And that *was* all. He really didn't mean a thing to me. Nothing. But I just couldn't understand how he could get himself in a situation like this one. It didn't make any sense. Squillante was a guy who started out as a numbers runner and worked his way to the top. He probably had the usual scraps but he was not what you would call a violent individual. He had something like 50 runners working for him. Figure each of them is making $150 a day. He's getting 10 percent of $150 times 50 runners, which is $750 per day. Plus he's got his own customers off who he's getting 35 percent. You figure he is doing maybe $250 a day with his own customers. Every fucking day. That's $1000 a day, $6000 a week. What is he ripping other people off for? I wanted to find out, so I asked the man who knew. "Jackie, I don't understand it. What the fuck is he doing it for? This guy is making a nice living."

"He went bad. For the last eight months he's been betting like the sun isn't coming up tomorrow. We've been checking with the books. We got hold of some of their runners and they tabbed Squillante as a heavy gambler. Since these robberies started though, he's been paying his bills very quickly."

"How much is he down?"

"We stopped counting at two hundred gees."

"Poor old Joe. He shoulda stayed in college."

Jackie shook his head no. "He should've stayed smart."

"Okay," I agreed.

He changed the subject. "What's your figure?" This part was more of a formality than anything else. There is a going rate for heavyweight work. The only time the price varies is when somebody big is going to be done. Squillante was nobody big. This was not going to be a bargaining session.

"Twenty thousand."

He reached into the inside pocket of his jacket and pulled out an envelope. "Here's the cash." I always get paid in full, in advance, in cash. What else am I gonna do, take a check? There are other unwritten clauses that go into every hit contract. Jackie and I didn't bother discussing them because we both knew what they were: If I got caught the Fat Man would be responsible for all my legal fees, including lawyers' fees and bail bonds if I could get bail. He would also see that I was comfortable in jail, that my wife was comfortable at home, as well as do everything possible to get me out. Finally, when I did get out, he would have a bundle of cash waiting for me.

This is done to insure silence. As long as all obligations are taken care of, I'm not going to say a word to nobody. I am certainly not going to involve Sweetlips or the Fat Man or Petey. All I can do by that is lose.

"I need all the information you got on him," I said. "I want his stops. I want a list of every runner he's got and where he meets them. I want his girlfriend if you got it. I want to know where he hangs out. Everything you got."

"You'll have everything you need tomorrow afternoon. We've been putting it together for the last week."

"Wonderful," I said, putting the envelope away. "I'll be at Aqueduct tomorrow. I'll be at the hundred-dollar window before the sixth race." I knew I would be there because there was an animal with whom I was deeply in love. "Make sure the party who brings the information is well known to me."

Jackie said, "He will be, because it'll be me. I don't want no goofs and I don't want no hassles."

"Any chance he's going to run?"

"No way. He thinks he's sitting on a gold mine."

"Yeah, but Jackie, this guy is not stupid. He must know you're gonna get on to him eventually," I said.

"What can I tell you? We just told his boys to tell him they can't do any jobs for two weeks. They agreed."

"Nice of them."

"Isn't it," he agreed.

Although I had been told this was to be a dinner meet, I didn't want to stay with this man. Just before I got up I asked him the one question that, in view of what he thought of me and what I thought of him, was bothering me.

"How come I got the contract?"

Sweetlips shrugged his shoulders. "Beats me. Petey told the Fat Man you're an angel. The Fat Man told me to get you."

I nodded. It sounded good enough. I got up to leave. "I'll see you tomorrow."

"All right," he said. As I started walking away he said one more thing. "Joey?" I turned.

"Yeah?"

"This time," he said, "you follow what I tell you, huh?"

I didn't say a word, I just walked out. Jackie Sweet-lips had not forgotten.

SWEETLIPS GIVES ME
THE ENVELOPE

If everything went according to plan—my plan—Joseph Squillante would become the 29th man I killed. Twenty-nine. That number in itself did not make me feel proud, and it didn't make me feel sad. Just cautious. The fact that I had killed 28 men and never been convicted of anything is no guarantee that I won't make some stupid mistake the 29th time and end up growing a long beard in the Graybar. In fact, one of the real problems with having done a lot of hits is that you can easily become overconfident.

The toughest moment in any hit man's career is pulling the trigger on number one. But that is much more of a mental thing than a physical thing. It takes almost no strength at all to pull a trigger. Anyone can do it. Kids, women, old people, everyone. But pointing it at someone's head and then pulling it is a different matter. There are simply not that many people in the world who will do that. (I'm not including the hysterically angry ones shooting their wives and like that.) But once you've done it, once you've seen a bullet disappear into someone's skull and watched with fascination as the whole pineapple opens up, once you've experienced how easy and quick it is, then there is absolutely nothing to it.

It actually becomes too easy. You begin to think of yourself in a different way. You feel you are somehow protected, that nothing can ever go wrong, that you are a very special person. This is a wonderful feeling if you know how to use it. Unfortunately, a lot of people don't know how to use it. They become too cocky. They get the idea they are untouchable. And so they get stupid and they get touched. But real professionals, people like me who treat this work as nothing more than a job, we rarely get this way. We stay careful. That way we stay in circulation.

Before I make a hit I go into every possible detail, every potential difficulty. I plan even the easiest job down to the final minute. I take notes and I make alternate plans. I work at my job the way a matador or dynamite truck driver works at his. Very carefully.

Even then I have made mistakes. I've been seen pulling the trigger. I've been seen in the areas where my bodies were found. These things happen, they're almost unavoidable if you work regularly. But I have never been convicted of anything because I was always ready for the possibility that something could happen. I've always played completely by the rules. I've always made sure I was working for legitimate people who would back me when I needed them. And, they did. The witnesses who said they saw me weren't sure they saw me, and the people who said I was in the area decided maybe I wasn't. I like to say that the people I worked for made sure that these so-called witnesses told the truth: First we decided what the truth is, then they told it.

On the surface, the Squillante job did not look like

it was going to be a difficult one. I had the complete cooperation of the people who hired me. I was going to have all the information available. The man had no idea he had become the bullseye. And I had as much time as I needed to fulfill the contract.

But, the more I thought about it, the more uncomfortable I felt. Why should the Fat Man, and Jackie, put Squillante on a $20,000 platter for *me?* I hadn't worked for them in over three years. Jackie had no love for me. And there are a *few* other good hit men around. I would guess that it might have something to do with the fact that I knew Squillante—it's always a plus to know the man you're after because you can get close to him easily—but there really is no way any of them could know that I knew him. And, of course, Petey was a friend and a fan of mine.

I filed these thoughts in the back of my mind. I decided to ask Petey what went on at the meeting where my name was brought up. And I also decided to keep an eye on my flanks. Further than that I couldn't afford to dwell on what-might-be. I had a job to do.

Loosely figuring, I gave Joseph Squillante two weeks to live.

The race meet was at Aqueduct at this time because the renovation of Belmont was underway. It didn't make much difference to me, I can lose my money at one place just as good as I can at another. Actually, except for the fact that it was all of a sudden very cold, it was not such a bad day. I had a couple of winners early and I was a few hundred bucks ahead at the end of the fifth race. I went up to the $100 window and waited. Sweetlips was precisely on time.

He walked up to me and handed me an envelope. "I got a present for you," he said.

"I thank you," I told him and stuck the envelope inside my pocket. I decided to be a little friendly. "You gonna stick around for awhile?"

He shook his head no. "Man, I book 'em, I don't bet 'em."

I laughed out loud. "I book 'em too."

"Yeah," he said, "I know." And he didn't laugh. Then he simply walked away, leaving without so much as a wave goodbye. I took a few short steps to the window and put my money down. If I had been a bit smarter I would have done what Sweetlips hadn't—waved goodbye.

This was my last visit to the track before really going to work. When I'm on a hit that's where I focus my attention. Of course, it's not the only thing I do—you got to keep your other businesses going—but I do try to stay away from the track. You've got enough things going without spending time studying the form.

After I left Aqueduct, about even for the day which was a pleasant change, I called my bookmaking office and got the week's results. At that point I was working a half-sheet, which means that I split all profits with the office, but that they covered all losses and took whatever they were down out of my future earnings. They told me I was ahead $6000 for the week. That means I had what is called a "black sheet." Of that $6000, I keep $3000 and the office gets the other half. All I have to do is collect it. I don't even have to visit the office, I simply go to my losers first and collect their debts, then pay the winners off out of that.

On the way to see my first loser, I stopped at my attorney's office and handed him $10,000 cash from the money Jackie gave me. He would put it in a safe-deposit box for me, and hold the key. The only people in the world who know about that box are my wife, my brother, my lawyer and me. If anything happens to me the money goes to my wife, my brother will see to that. Besides, I trust this lawyer in financial matters. You have to trust someone.

I spent a good portion of the afternoon going around visiting my customers. I meet most of them at their offices, at bars, at restaurants. Sometimes they just leave the money with a bartender or maître d', but they manage to get it to me somehow.

I started with my losers. I am used to losers. A man who has lost for the week will usually be grumpy and say things like, "I'm gonna get you next week," or, "Boy, were you lucky this week," or the most familiar, "If only I had listened to my brother-in-law who had a friend who knew this guy who knew this jockey's butcher . . ." But most of your losers pay up right away. Only occasionally do you get somebody who has gone in over his head and can't pay, a Joseph Squillante for instance.

I have had my share of welchers. No one as deep as Squillante, but I have had people go close to $100,000. I'll let them go if they have a good job and good standing, because I know they'll find some way to pay me back, if not in cash, in services. I had free use of a 1973 Cadillac Coupe de Ville all year thanks to a car dealer who fell behind. Instead of letting the "vig," the interest, add up each week, he just let me have the car while paying back the principal. There's a term for this. It's called life insurance.

One way or another I had seen or gotten in touch with everyone with one exception. All of a sudden it's 6:30 and Solly from the garment district isn't anywhere around. I had nicknamed him Sorry Solly because he had been losing pretty consistently and at this point was down about $3000. This is not really much because I know Solly has his own importing firm and I know he's worth a lot more than that. But he had been putting me off for a few weeks and promised he would be able to settle on this particular afternoon. I don't get mad, I just make a mental note to call him tomorrow and see what his story is.

After finishing with my losers I meet my winners. They are *always* gonna be there in person! Winners are just as predictable as losers. Every winner is convinced he has finally learned the secret of successful gambling and from this point on he will never have another losing week. Fine, I encourage that. I want them betting with me.

I got a doctor from the Bronx who bets with me. I'll stop by his office on Monday or Tuesday and, if he's a winner, which he is often enough, he'll be screaming and shouting, "I got you this time. You'll never see this money again."

"Not until next week," is my usual, and usually accurate reply. I swear, this guy would rather hit an exacta than find the cure for cancer. I like him as a customer, but if I was sick I wouldn't go near him with a cold.

I never meet all my customers every week. Normally, if a guy has a break-even week, or if he's just a few dollars ahead or behind, we'll let it ride another week and put it on his account. On this particular night I was home by 10:30 P.M.

My old lady was not on the premises when I arrived, which is not at all unusual. This is one remarkable woman. She knew all about women's liberation long before them other big mouths started shooting off. But more importantly, she understood how to handle it. Because of my profession I have a somewhat erratic schedule called no schedule at all. Sometimes I'll be home for dinner, sometimes not. Sometimes I'll leave town for a few days on very little notice. This woman takes everything in perfect stride. She has a complete life of her own—but she manages to incorporate my life into it.

I didn't know exactly where she was this evening. She might have been out playing Mah-jongg or canasta or bridge or at the movies with some of her girlfriends. The one thing I know she wasn't doing was seeing another man. That is just about the only thing I would not stand for. I've treated that woman superwonderful. She has more money salted away than the Green Giant has peas. And I also give her the respect that a husband owes to his wife. I know how lucky I am.

My first wife was killed because I was involved in illegitimate enterprises. I was hauling drugs into the country for an independent operator. It was all very easy, I was just taping the packages to the rims of my car tires. The customs people might inspect the tire, but they never take it off the rim. I had done enough work to be owed $40,000, but this wise guy thought it would be cheaper to kill me. Which it would have been, had he been successful. He hired three thugs to do this job, and they went to my house when I wasn't home. My wife, who was very pregnant at the time, let them in. Instead of being gentlemen and leaving when they saw I wasn't there, they kicked her in the stomach, and then left her lying there. She hemorrhaged and died.

I hunted each of the three thugs down and killed

them very slowly and very painfully. The boss was luckier—he was arrested and sent to jail. When he comes out, if he lives that long, I'm going to kill him too.

I appreciate my second wife. I appreciate the things she does for me. For example, this night I appreciated the fact that she wasn't home. I sat myself down in my big print-covered easy chair, turned the light on and opened the envelope Jackie Sweetlips had given me. There, on a piece of paper neatly typed, was everything I always wanted to know about Joseph Squillante but never bothered to ask.

There were four pages filled with information about Squillante: where he lived, background about his family life, where they went on their vacation the previous summer (Disneyland!), even his middle name (Franklin). Also his car, the type, color, license-plate number and even the fact that it had a big scratch on the right rear fender. They also gave me the name and address of his girlfriend and his best friend, an advertising executive who had nothing to do with the business. Finally there was a list of additional items of information about his haunts and habits. The thing that attracted my attention most was the line that said, "As far as is known, Squillante does not carry any weapon. No one has ever seen him handling a gun."

The last two pages gave me his normal daily schedule and the information I needed about his runners: where they lived, their phone numbers and where Squillante picked up from them. The office had this information in case something happened to Squillante and someone had to fill in for him. When what was going to happen to Squillante happened, someone, probably one of his runners, would inherit this list.

The names were not listed in any particular order,

but they were grouped by general geographical location. There was also a little notation next to each one, indicating whether they figured to be early or late pick-ups. Three or four were called "possible last pick-ups." The reason the office knew that is because Squillante would occasionally call or stop in at the bank before finishing for the day and say, "I'll be back in a half hour because I've got to stop and pick up from so-and-so."

Squillante would start picking up his numbers by 8 A.M. at the latest. This did not thrill me because I knew I would have to get up very early to beat this bird. The list did not say where the runners were picking up their action, but they would meet him in the Bronx. By 10:30 he would have picked up approximately 45 envelopes and then drive downtown with the money and the slips to the bank, to drop everything off. Then he would go back and meet his final runners. Two days a week, at least, he would not go to the bank first. Instead he would keep the action with him and go to his girlfriend's place. She was a Puerto Rican girl who lived in the Randall Projects up in Throgs Neck. She had one kid, a little boy, seven years old.

According to the list he generally turned everything in and had all his paperwork done by 2 P.M., 2:30 at the latest. Since the numbers is based on total mutuel betting, all bets are supposed to be in the office by the time the first race goes off. Since it had gotten cold they were starting the animals at 12:30, so I figured old Joe would be done by 1:30. Then, at some point he would stop in at the office to pick up his results, and the cash for his winners.

So this list told me a lot about Squillante. The only thing it didn't explain, was how the hell could he have gotten in so deep? He owed more than $200,000! That means he had probably lost another $300–400,000 before that and had paid off. I didn't understand it.

The thing that amazes me about Squillante and people like him is that they know what a sucker game this is, and they know very few people ever come out ahead. Squillante had more tax-free dollars than he ever dreamed of, yet he got fucking desperate. I make big money. I gamble. I lose, and I blow a lot of money. But I never bet more than is in my pocket. I have never yet made a fucking bet if I couldn't cover it. I have never borrowed money unless I knew I could pay it back and when I could pay it back. It amazes me that people in my business could leave themselves in a position to get shafted. Or that they would get greedy and steal. And Squillante? Doing both? I found it hard to understand. And even harder to believe.

I was trying to digest as much of the material as I could before my wife came home and found me sitting there reading. My wife has seen me do a lot of unusual things in the time we've been together, but reading is not often one of them. If I had anything besides a racing form or the *New York Daily News* in my hand she would know something unusual was happening and I didn't need that nohow.

She came wandering in at 12:30. By that point I knew as much about Squillante as the Fat Man and Jackie Sweetlips, and was deeply immersed in the Johnny Carson Show. She was thrilled because she was a winner for the night. The game was Mah-jongg and the last of the great riverboat hustlers had won herself a sparkling $1.78 or something like that. I had a better surprise for her.

"How about some coffee?" I asked her.

"That's a good idea," she agreed, "you make it."

"I'll tell you what," I bargained, "you make it and I'll give you a surprise."

She looked directly at me. "You going away again?"

I didn't like her sense of humor. "Ha, ha," I answered. "Just put some hot water up, okay? And don't give me a hard time." This time she did exactly that.

She served it to me in the living room. "Where's my surprise?"

I handed her the envelope. It had $5000 in it. "Here," I said. "If you made better coffee you could have had more." I laughed. I always make it a point to give my wife a chunk of whatever I earn. It keeps her happy, and when she's happy she doesn't give me a hard time, so I'm happy. It also keeps her loyal. And she deserves it. So, $5000 for her, $10,000 in the safe-deposit box and $5000 for me and Aqueduct to share.

She smiled as she counted it. I don't know what she does with her money, I never ask, but she must have a sizable amount stashed away somewhere. "Thank you very much," she said and kissed me on the forehead. She never asked me where it came from. She suspects what I do, but I don't believe she actually *knows* that I pull the trigger. That's the way I want it. And that's the way she wants it also.

I don't think she would have taken the money if she knew it was partial payment for the death of Joe Squillante.

The countdown had begun.

TAILING HIM

I am not a morning person. Some people are actually sharper in the morning than they are at night. I am not one of those people. I think it goes back to when I was a kid just starting out and I had to get up at 5 A.M. and go stand on a corner to take numbers bets from people on their way to work. It always seemed to be cold and I was usually very tired. So when I started doing good financially I reserved the mornings for sleeping. In fact, if I do have to get up early in the morning, I'm usually awake a half-hour before my heart starts beating.

If there is one thing I dislike more than early mornings, it is cold early mornings. There is a chill that just cuts right through you, no matter how much clothing you have on. This Tuesday morning was damn cold out, so naturally I was not at all thrilled at getting up at 6 A.M. to go chase Joe Squillante all over the Bronx. But business is business. You got a job to do, you get up and you do it. And I had a job to do.

The only tools I had with me when I left the house and climbed into my sparkling 1966 Oldsmobile Cutlass were maps of the Bronx and Manhattan, two pens, a notepad, a portable radio, a wristwatch and an army blanket. I didn't even carry a gun with me, although there was one safely tucked away behind a false back in the glove compartment. I don't like to carry a piece on me unless I have to—for example, I would never go to any sort of meeting without a loaded weapon— and in this particular case it didn't seem to be necessary. The gun in the glove compartment is for emergencies. None of which requiring that kind of solution have ever come up.

The reasons for the maps were obvious. Even though I know every street in the Bronx like I know every wrinkle on my wife, I really wanted to pinpoint my location in terms of one-way streets, traffic lights, construction obstructions, stop signs and blocks closed because of children at play. I was planning to make these notations on the map as we went along. The pad was for writing down thoughts and ideas about certain places; what made them desirable, acceptable or no damn good. The portable radio was to preserve my battery when I was just sitting there, watching and waiting. The wristwatch was because, as expected, the clock in the car did not work. The blanket again is obvious—it gets damn fucking cold sitting in a car without the heater on. And I can't turn the heater on because it won't work if the engine isn't on and I can't turn the engine on because I've got to save gas because I never know how long I'm going to be sitting in one spot.

In order to see what Squillante's schedule was like I had to be at his house before he left for his morning's work. I got to his place, which was just off Roberts Avenue, about a quarter of seven. He was walking out of his front door just as I got there. If I had been five minutes later I would have missed him. He was dressed for the weather, a leather coat that looked to be lined, a scarf and a hat. The hat I expected. Squillante is one of the few hat people I know. When we were teen-agers he was the first individual who wore a suit on any day except Sunday. The guy always liked to dress good, and I guess wearing a hat is part of that. This particular hat was very advertising-man. Gray, brim bending slightly over his forehead and one little multicolored feather sticking out of the side. If you didn't know he was going to pick up from his runners you might guess he was on his way to a law office or some such place.

He was driving a white 1966 Buick. Nothing special, but nice enough. You'll notice few guys making a lot of money within the structure of organized crime drive flashy cars or live expensively. People who spend their days driving around in limousines and their nights in expensive clubs are prime picking for the Internal Revenue Service. And there is no need to attract unnecessary attention.

He pulled out of his parking spot on the street and headed toward Westchester Avenue. I waited a few seconds, then took off after him. The point of following somebody is never to let them out of your sight, but to stay out of their sight as much as possible. There are only a few ways of doing this—for example, you always drive to the rear right of the man you're trailing. That way he won't constantly see you in his rear-view mirror. And, most importantly, you never, never stay with your man for too long at one time. If you do, he is eventually going to pick you up. I had no intention of staying with him for more than an hour or two. I just wanted to get the feel of him the first day.

His first stop was at a restaurant right at the end of Westchester Avenue by the Pelham Bay station. He parked his car in front of a hydrant, walked in and had what looked like a cup of coffee. I was sitting across the street and could not see inside so well. As he walked out two guys came up to him and handed him envelopes.

From the restaurant he proceeded down the Bruckner Expressway, then he cut over to Tremont Avenue. He made a right onto Tremont and then drove straight down to the Middletown Avenue cut-off. He stopped by a subway entrance over there, met a guy and picked up an envelope. Then he drove to Westchester Square and picked up another envelope. From there he went south on Westchester until he reached St. Lawrence and there were three guys standing there to meet him. He took their envelopes.

This is going boom-boom-boom. His stops never lasted more than a few seconds and it was obvious he was on a very tight schedule. He really had his schedule worked out well, his runners were always there to meet him and he did not have to wait. Most of them had picked up their action during the night from the pimps, prostitutes, people on their way to work, cab drivers, hustlers and late-shift cops. The day action, from the shop owners, housewives and day workers who bet at work, would come in later in the morning and early afternoon.

From St. Lawrence he went over to Watson Avenue and White Plains and met two colored guys. Then he went down Watson to Rosedale Avenue and found a place to park, again in front of a hydrant. He walked into the project with a brown manila-type envelope under his arm—obviously where he kept his slips and collections. He went into one building and was there about 30 seconds and then he came out and walked across the courtyard into a second building. Again,

30 seconds later he's out and I see he's got maybe six envelopes in his hand and he's stuffing them in the brown manila. This was obviously all the action from the project which, I assure you, can be quite substantial.

With those envelopes in hand, he got on the Pelham Parkway and went up to the Pelham Bay station. He stopped and walked into a restaurant called The Six Brothers and saw two guys. He walked out of there and up the block into another restaurant where he saw three different guys, although I couldn't be sure he collected from all of them. He was really hustling now. From the second restaurant he went across the street into a candy store where two guys were waiting for him. Then he got back into his car and drove over to Allerton Avenue. All this time I'm trying to follow him and take as many notes as I can. At this point I'm not even stopping to consider what locations might be good for the hit and which ones can be immediately eliminated. I'm just following and writing, following and writing.

He stopped at Allerton and Barker. Another car pulled up next to him and a guy leaned over and handed him a number of envelopes. Then my boy drove east up Allerton to the intersection of Allerton and Boston Road. Then over to Allerton and Wallace. There is a big supermarket there and he parked in the lot and went inside. I gotta assume he saw someone in there.

From that point he began heading into the southeast Bronx. He went over to Tremont and Southern Boulevard and met somebody there. Next stop was in the Hunts Point section, which made me happy. Hunts Point is perhaps the toughest section in the Bronx and has long been a good dumping ground for used bodies.

He stopped in front of the Loews Spooner Theatre. There were four colored guys waiting for him in front of the theatre and they reached into the car and dropped envelopes into his manila carrying case. Then he turned down Hunts Point Avenue to Lafayette I think it was, and met a big fat colored woman who handed him an envelope. Where she collected from I don't know. Maybe in one of the big factories in the area.

He parked about a block later, again in front of a hydrant—the man has absolutely no respect for the law—and went into four of the factories. These are particularly profitable markets for a good runner because all these places have a lot of employees and they all bet. All of them.

From there he went back into the Bronx, up by Castle Hill Avenue. There is a big envelope factory there and he met three people.

By this time it's 10 A.M. and I am getting really tired and bored. Not careless though, I never forget that I'm on a job and one mistake is one more than I can afford. I followed him to a coffee shop on 174th and either Bryant Avenue or Vise Avenue. He sat there and began reading his paper and making some phone calls. I didn't know whether he was calling his bookie, which I doubted because he really hadn't had time to study the form, or what he was doing. I really could not care less because I decided that I had had enough for one day and was going to move along. Having worked in this business many years I know that controllers are creatures of habit—of necessity— and so I was pretty positive that Squillante's morning schedule was not going to change too much from day to day. I figured it would be very easy for me to pick him up right at this coffee shop Wednesday morning.

I was really tired myself by this time and decided to grab a cup of coffee and maybe a danish. Since I had no plans for a few hours I drove into Manhattan to a luncheonette owned and operated by a friend of mine named Johnny Dee. Johnny Dee is the funniest man I have ever known in my life. He will say anything to anybody, particularly his customers. I once heard him tell a woman giving him grief to "go out and get hit by a bus, you old geezer," and the look on her face broke me up.

He really didn't care if his customers ever came in again or not, because the place was actually a combination luncheonette and bookmaking business. He had only one phone and maybe 20 customers who used it, but he did very fine. So he didn't care as much as I did if his danish turned out to be three days old.

As I walked in he was taking down a round-robin. He was very serious when booking bets, these customers he did not fool around with. "What do you have that's fresh?" I asked him as he hung up.

"A fourteen-year-old daughter," he said.

I laughed. "What's happening tough guy?"

"Nixon and Humphrey, Nixon and Humphrey," he said. "All my customers want me to find them someone to take their bet. What do I look like?"

"A bookmaker," I told him.

"Animals and athletes only," he corrected me. "I don't book no presidents. Can't figure 'em, can't trust 'em. Give me the horses every time. They give you an honest day's work for a bale of hay." This was just as the 1968 elections were heating up. Nixon had jumped off to a big lead but Humphrey was making his move into the stretch. "Who you voting for?" he asked me.

I gave him an empty look. "One's a crook and the other's a bum. Which one do you think?" As I said that I poured myself a cup of his so-called coffee and asked, "What's on the menu this morning?"

He picked one up and looked at it. "It looks like a dead roach to me."

I took two of his semi-stale danish and retired to a booth in the back. I took out my pad and began studying the information I had compiled. I cross-checked it with the material Jackie had given me and from what I could see Squillante had picked up about 40 envelopes. A good, solid morning's work.

For the first time I began to think about when and where I might make my move. I had absolutely no preconceived ideas about either question. The only time an individual does have to decide beforehand is when he goes to another town and he's told this location would be particularly good, or this and that location are suitable. If you know the city you really should not depend on other people.

I hadn't even decided day or night. Although nighttime is usually preferable, it's not always possible. If a man makes a habit of spending his nights in front of the television set you can forget about it. No one is going to sit in front of his house until he gets the urge to wander out and then take a random shot at him. You're not if you have a brain in your cranium. So you study every possibility.

I went down my list very carefully and next to each spot which I thought might have potential I wrote down "OK." Then I know this is a place I want to come back and look at again later. Next to the places that didn't seem to hold too much hope—the project he visited for instance—I wrote down "No," and made a thin line through the area.

The place that looked the very best at first glance was Hunts Point. Hunts Point is actually the world's

largest sewer. At one time it had been a major indus-
trial area and, although it was still busy, a lot of business moved out when the junkies, pimps and hookers
moved in. Hunts Point had a lot going for it: There
are wide open areas, there is noise, and there are
enough people around doing strange things that nobody looks to butt into anybody else's business. With
a silencer, if I could catch him by himself, Hunts
Point could be the place. And there are a few moments when he is by himself, out of view of all his
runners. Finally I made a little asterisk next to it. Although it wasn't perfect, of the places I had seen today it was the best.

While I am studying these sheets Johnny is screaming up a storm at a nonexistent repairman who is not
sitting on a stool in front of his counter. "You son-of-
a-bitch," he yelled, "I call you for four days to get in
here and fix this spritzer and where the hell are you?
I hope your fuckin' truck gets a flat tire on 125th
Street at three o'fucking clock in the morning!"

"See you, Johnny."

"Where you going without paying? You owe me
seventy cents. Twenty for the coffee and a quarter
each for the danish. What kind of establishment do
you think I'm running where you can walk out without paying?"

"Seventy cents for that shit?" I screamed as loudly
as he did. "For weak coffee and two stale danish?
That's highway robbery!"

"You want first-class service you pay for it!" So I
paid for it. I got even though, I didn't leave him no tip.

That same afternoon I began to gather the equipment I would need. In other words, I made arrangements to get myself a gun.

Getting a gun in New York City is about as difficult as finding a hooker in Las Vegas. I can go anywhere in New York and get myself a gun within 24 hours. The only difficulty is making sure you get a perfectly clean weapon, one which cannot be traced back to you, or traced back to the individual you got it from in the first place. An entire gun-supply industry has developed in New York. There are a number of people in this city who make a nice few extra dollars supplying clean guns and asking no questions. Perhaps the best of them all is Cockeyed Jimmy.

Cockeyed Jimmy and I have known each other since we were kids. He's a good thief and from time to time we did things together. He stands about 6'4" and weighs a solid 250 without any fat, and he looks bigger. Jimmy became known as Cockeyed about 20 years ago when he tried to ball a nightclub singer— right in the middle of her act. When the nightclub toughs tried to prevent this union, Jimmy kayoed four of them and went a good way towards wrecking the place. Love has no greater actor than a 6'4" muscleman with the hots.

After that people kept saying, "Watch out for that guy, he's cockeyed," so they hung the name on him. I enjoyed working with him. At one point we were doing a little muscle work for a bookmaking outfit and we went to visit this businessman who was not paying his bills as regularly as he should've. The first time we went to see him his secretary told us he was in a meeting and could not be disturbed.

We returned the next day and, again, his secretary tried to put us off. I opened the door to his office with a good, swift kick and in we went. He was sitting behind his desk and when he looked up and saw us he turned as white as if he had just seen Attila the Hun and his elephant walk in the door. "Listen, stupid," I said, "if you want to jerk people around, it's always better to talk to them first."

I don't know where this guy got the courage, but he opened his mouth and blurted out, "I'll pay when I damn well feel like it!"

Finally Cockeyed Jimmy opened his mouth. "You will?" he asked casually. This was one of the older buildings in which you could actually open the windows. We weren't very high up, but we were high enough that a man would make a nice splat if he fell from that height. Jimmy went over and opened the window. We had no more intention of throwing him out the window than we did of mugging his kids, but he didn't know that. We picked him up and started carrying him toward the window.

He started screaming bloody murder, "My heart, my heart. I got a bad heart!"

"Think of it this way," Jimmy answered. "You won't have to worry about your heart no more."

"I'll pay ya, I'll pay ya." He wrote out a check and the three of us walked to the bank and cashed it.

Jimmy had shifted operations to the docks a long time ago. He was a longshoreman with a reputation as big as he was for making things happen. Everybody on the docks knows him, so it is never any trouble locating him.

I drove over to West 45th Street and stopped the first longshoreman I met. "Hey," I asked, "you know Cockeyed Jimmy?"

"What about him?"

"You seen him?" He said he hadn't. "Well, listen, if you do see him you tell him Joey's up at the Market Diner on Fifty-first and Twelfth and he wants to see him." Longshoremen have one of the tightest and most effective codes in the world. They look out for one another. If you give one guy a message you can usually be sure it will get where it is supposed to get. And, just as important, no one will be able to remember how it got there.

The word was indeed passed quickly. By the time I got to the diner, ordered a cup of coffee, flipped through the *Daily News* and the songs on the little juke box in the booth, Cockeyed Jimmy walked in. He crossed the whole place in maybe four long strides and stuck out that ham he calls a hand. "What's doing kid, how are you?" I told him and we bullshitted each other for a few minutes to catch up on old times and old people. Eventually we got around to business. "Whattya need?"

"Some goods," I said. "A piece and a silencer to match."

He nodded. "You got it."

"What's the tab?" This was not like Johnny Dee's place, where maybe I walk out without paying. This is a cash money deal.

"The piece is seventy-five and the silencer is two hundred." Just about what I expected. Cockeyed Jimmy is known to be fast and reasonable. There are people who will try to charge you as much as $600 for a silencer. And, in fact, you may never use it. A silencer cuts the sound of a gun discharging from BAM to bim. In some places, hit number 28 for example, you don't want to use it at all. You want to attract attention. But at this point I didn't know where I was going to do Squillante.

"Okay. That's fair. When can I get it?"

"I'll have it for you in two hours. Where you gonna be?"

"Call me at Patsy's Restaurant." The whole meet

took ten minutes, and I had myself a gun and silencer on the way.

Patsy's is the best Italian restaurant in New York City. It's a joint on First Avenue and 108th Street frequented by connoisseurs of fine cuisine. By the time I meandered my way up there Jimmy had already called once. No problem, I know he's going to call back. So I sit down and finish reading the paper, have a slice of pie, sit with the owner for awhile and sure enough the phone rings and it's for me.

"How are you?" says Cockeyed Jimmy.

"Still shittin' bricks." He just wanted to make sure it was me.

"Wonderful," he said. "Your bird is here."

"Is it domestic or imported?"

"We got you a domestic one."

I said, "Very good," emphasizing the *very*. When I order a gun I don't order anything specific unless I know I need a certain weapon. So I'll get whatever my supplier can steal. It could be a .32, .38, .45, he's got to check the crates on the docks and see what is around.

Jimmy gets his supplies from a number of different places, but his main source is the crates of guns either being imported or exported, and just waiting on the docks. I would wager there isn't a crate of guns that comes in or out of New York without a few items missing. (This was in 1968, before the heavy supply of the so-called Saturday Night Specials started coming in from the surrounding states.)

In this particular case Jimmy obtained for me a .38, which is fine because that is the weapon I almost always use. Jimmy told me to get into my car and meet him under the West Side Highway at 20th Street. He was standing there when I pulled up.

"Here's the toy," he said, handing me a brown paper bag. "I'll have your silencer either tonight or tomorrow. Call me later at the number I wrote on the bag."

"You do good work my friend. I'll speak to you." Normally about this time of the week I'm beginning to put my cigarette deals together. And I have been playing with the thought of going ahead and sending a truck down but I know this is going to take a lot of my time and thought. I've got to do everything from borrow the cash to make the purchases from Joe Cheese to hire the kids to distribute the goods when they arrive. All this time should be spent thinking about Joe Squillante. Too much, just too much. I finally decided to screw it for the week—although my two new customers are going to be unhappy—because there is no reason to hurt both operations by splitting my time.

During this whole period I had not spent too much time with my wife. Except for an occasional fight we never just sat down and talked, so I decided I would give her a surprise. I would beat her home and cook a nice dinner for her. Cooking is one of my true hobbies. I love to put on my apron that my brother gave me which says, "Please do not bother the chef. He is doing the best job he can," and really cook us a super dish.

The biggest decision of my day is what I'm going to make: The winner is meatballs and Italian sauce. Joey's special Italian sauce, guaranteed to make your mouth water and burn your eyes out! On the way home I stopped at the market and picked up tomatoes, some spices, a chunk of pork for flavoring and some chop meat. This is going to be a nice surprise.

Unfortunately, my wife had a surprise of her own. "Tonight you are taking me to Macy's!"

I started to argue but then she started reeling off a list of presents we owed to various people and how she was so embarrassed and on and on. So she broiled some hot dogs, opened a can of beans, and off we went to Manhattan and the world's largest department store.

I don't particularly enjoy shopping, and I hate big crowds, but I've never minded going to Macy's. When we were growing up in the middle of the depression Macy's always had a special meaning. Occasionally I would go down there with a group of friends and we would just wander through the store, wide eyed and bushy tailed. just looking at all the things we couldn't afford. We'd steal if we could, but that was never the reason we went down. We went down to see what the other side of the tracks was like. So now, even when we can afford Bloomingdale's and Bonwit's and other places like that, most of the people from the old neighborhood are still loyal to Macy's.

We started in the electronics department. My nephew was about to have either his 16th or 17th birthday and my wife wanted to buy him a clock-radio. $39.95.

Up to linens. A wedding present for the daughter of one of her close friends. $28 plus tax.

Into housewares. An anniversary gift for a couple I could never stand. Some sort of broiler plate. $16.99.

Finally my wife said, "Now I want to get some pants for myself." Like a good husband I followed her into the women's department. And like a good husband I stood in the corner and minded my own business while she waded into the midst of the display racks. And it was while I was standing there, slowly eliminating the beans from my system, that I met another good husband.

Joseph Franklin Squillante!

I didn't even see him coming. All of a sudden I heard my name called out and I turned around and there was the entire family: the victim-to-be, his wife and their three children.

I did my very best to put a wide smile on my face. "Hey, Joe, how you doin'?"

"Wonderful, fine," he said, "everything's goin' good." As usual he was well dressed. As usual, he had a hat on. And Cindy, his wife, looked better than ever. I could have sworn her tits were growing upwards, but her waist seemed just as small as it ever was. "What are you doin' here?"

I pointed over to my wife. "Spending money. And you?"

He nodded. "Same thing. I was just telling . . ." My wife spotted me talking to them and hurried over. She had met them before, a long time ago, but didn't really remember them. It didn't matter though, she immediately made friends with Cindy and before I realized what she was doing, she and Cindy were on their way to the toy department with the three Squillante children. And Joe and I were sitting down over a cup of coffee.

We quickly filled each other in on mutual friends. He told me: Jamie Goldberg was a doctor, Bart Rush was working in the garment center, Dugie Giancarlo was a cop and Buster Harrelson was coming up for sentencing on an assault rap.

I told him: Monk Campbell was a lawyer, Jughead we-couldn't-remember-his-last-name got killed in a car accident, and Tony DeLuca owned some sort of manufacturing plant. "You know, Joe," I said to him, "all things considered, the guys from the neighborhood did pretty good."

He agreed. "How about you Joey?" he asked me. "What are you doin' now?" Squillante knew I was in numbers and bookmaking and everything else I could get my hands into. And probably he'd heard that I did heavyweight work. But I was not about to tell him.

"I do whatever comes along Joe, just like always. I got a piece of a book downtown. Card game now and then, you know, I keep busy." I paused. "You still with the Fat Man?"

He smiled. "Yeah. Did I tell you that he made me a controller a few years ago?"

"Yeah. I heard that from somebody. You doing alright then?"

"Yeah. good," he said.

It was not really that strange sitting and talking with him. At least it wasn't once I had gotten over the initial shock of bumping into him. I've sat with people I knew were about to die a number of times before. Later I would be with Joey Gallo a number of times after I knew the contract on him was out. But there was one difference in being with Squillante: I was the gun.

After we finished the small talk I didn't know what to say. But after running it through my mind quickly I decided to use the occasion to do a little research. "Hey, how come I never see you at the tracks. I remember that you were the first guy on the block to buy the racing form."

He laughed. The guy had a big smile. I had forgotten he had such a big smile. "Whattya doin', lookin' for customers?"

I laughed. "Everywhere."

"Not me," he said, "who's got the time? I got a route to run every day. I never touch the horses. Can't afford it. I used to . . ."

I stopped listening. The man said he never touched the horses! That made absolutely no sense at all. Here was a guy supposedly $200,000 in debt from gambling and he's telling me he never goes near the nags. All of a sudden I had a queasy feeling in the pit of my stomach. Something was definitely rotten in the Bronx.

". . . me my lesson. No more. Not me."

I chuckled very uneasily. "Wish I could say the same."

We finished our coffee and went back to the toy department to meet the women. My old lady and Cindy had become bosom buddies, which was alright with me because I liked Cindy. They even exchanged phone numbers and there was some talk about getting together. I said I'd love to, lying a little. Things were definitely not going the way I expected. I was quiet on the way home.

"What's the matter with you?" my wife asked.

"I don't know yet," I told her. Then she shut up and let me think.

DOUBTS AND
GREAT DANES

On the way over to the coffee shop to pick up on Squillante the next morning I started going over the situation in my head. What it came down to was that I had been hired by a man who hated me, supposedly to do a job on an individual I knew, for doing what he says he isn't. There is only one conclusion I can reach: If Squillante isn't lying then maybe he isn't being the one set up for the kill.

Maybe I am.

It's happened before. I knew of a Jersey hit man who was hired to make a hit out in the swamps. He waited there a few hours and then his supposed victim showed up—with two other guys and a shitload of bullets. They left the hit man floating. It would not surprise me if Jackie Sweetlips had finally gained enough power to fulfill his wish about getting even with me. I knew Petey would never get involved in something like that, but it is possible he really doesn't know about the setup.

So maybe it's me instead of Squillante.

Or maybe it is Squillante and I'm letting my mind work too hard.

Or maybe it's both of us.

I really had no choice about what to do. I couldn't confront Jackie or the Fat Man. What would they tell me? That I'm the target? No way. I couldn't turn the job down, I had already taken the money. So my decision was to continue to follow Squillante, get the job done as soon as possible, and keep an eye to the rear right of my car.

And I started carrying a loaded .38 inside my belt.

I arrived at the coffee shop and sat outside in my car waiting. I briefly toyed with the idea of going in and getting a cup of coffee and bringing it outside, but I didn't want to take the chance on Squillante walking in on me. If this thing was legitimate, I had to figure Squillante must be at least a little itchy, and seeing me twice in two days is more than a coincidence. The one thing I didn't want him to do was start getting paranoid. When a man starts getting itchy he starts getting erratic and unpredictable and that is precisely what I did not need. So I sat in my car and waited.

He showed up a few minutes after the hour and I watched through the window as he sat and had two cups of coffee and gabbed with an ugly waitress. I was just beginning to get angry with him for sitting there so long when we both got better things to do, when he finally decided to leave. The chase resumed.

He drove directly to the funeral home to bury all the envelopes and slips he had on him. I never understood why he did that because I knew from the list that he hadn't finished his collections. I wasn't at all surprised though, because Sweetlips had mentioned the possibility on his fact sheet. So far, in fact, that information had been perfect. Maybe, I wondered, even too perfect. But all I did was write the information down on my little pad.

He didn't stay there very long and from there we went back up to the Bronx. He made his first stop at a cab garage at 142nd Street and Jackson. Obviously the dispatcher there was collecting from his drivers and anyone else who wandered by during the night. This could be a highly profitable little business for the dispatcher. I have seen guys pulling in $500 per night just sitting in a garage if their drivers hustle and have customers of their own.

Squillante walked down the block to 141st and Jackson and hit a second cab garage. His third, and what turned out to be the final stop of his working day, was at Fordham Road and the Grand Concourse. There were three guys waiting for him with envelopes. Then he drove back to the bank again. While he was in the bank I cross-checked my list with Jackie's list and from what I could see we had covered all his runners. So that portion of his day was finished. Now came the cute part, trying to figure out some sort of pattern for what he did the rest of the day.

People who live and work within organized crime usually lead pretty unorganized lives after they've done their work for the day. It's tough to be able to predict what a guy is going to do three days from Tuesday when chances are the guy himself doesn't know. What you have to try to do is find some point to which he keeps returning: a girlfriend, a card game, a friend's apartment, a social club. And after you've got that, all you have to do is figure out when he'll be there. It is not easy.

Squillante stayed in the funeral home about 25 minutes, tying up his sheet and everything. He drove from there back up into the Bronx, to the project on Randall Avenue where his girlfriend lived. He got there about two o'clock and parked. I wanted to see how long he stayed there, so I parked too. There's no way of telling about a man and his girlfriend. Some guys will run to their girlfriend's house every day and stay for 20 minutes. just a quickie to tickle their fancy, or whatever else they're into. Others will make an entire day out of it. I figured Squillante would be there for awhile because he fancied himself a ladies' man and I knew he could never hit and run. It just wasn't in the man's character.

So I sat there waiting. And waiting. And waiting some more. I've always believed that waiting is the most difficult part of making a hit. You can overcome everything but boredom. You listen to the radio, you think, you try to pass the time someway, but each minute just drags on.

For the first time since I took the job, I started thinking about this Joseph Squillante. Assuming he *was* doing what they said he was doing, he certainly was not very uptight about it. He was floating around free and fancy. In fact, I thought a little too free for an individual who has got to be aware his life could be snapped off at any point. A guy who had hired two punks to rip off his employers—neither stupid nor gentle people! He didn't even seem to be looking over his shoulder. He seemed to be making my job very easy. Too easy.

I wondered what was going through his mind when he made the decision to double-cross the Fat Man. This is supposed to be a bright person, a year at City College. successful controller, how could he ever believe he would get away with it? I couldn't figure it out.

I wondered if he spent much time worrying about his debts. How could he not worry? Yet, when I met him at Macy's, he seemed not to be bothered at all. Another strange thought popped into my mind: In the brief time I had been following him I had not seen him make one move that looked like he was placing a bet. Not even one bet. I suppose he could have been making them from his girlfriend's apartment, but I would have been really surprised if he was going up to this chick's place to read the form or the sports pages, and he's not gonna bet if he doesn't peruse them might-tee care-fully. I knew he wasn't about to quit—I've never seen anybody quit when they were as far behind as he was, people at that stage are always looking to get even with one blow—but I hadn't seen him place a single bet yet. As soon as I saw him do that, I knew a lot of my doubts about this job would fade away. But I had to see it soon, or I would be getting uptight myself.

As I sat there I never took my eyes off the front door of her building. I wondered exactly where her apartment was. Sweetlips's fact sheet said 7N. I thought casually about checking it myself, but gave up that idea fast. Again, I didn't want to see Squillante again no how, no way. And I had been caught checking an apartment building once before. I knew it could easily happen again.

I was going to do this guy in Chicago. When I got there my employers gave me the entire layout. I said, "You don't mind if I check it out?" and they said of course not, go ahead. One of the locations they suggested was his girlfriend's apartment, so I went over there. I was walking into the hallway when he came down the stairs. I quickly began looking at the names and numbers listed next to the buzzers. He was very helpful. "You need some help?" he asked, not in the nicest tone but still an ask.

I didn't blink an eye. "I'm looking for Phil Lefkowitz. But I can't find his name on this thing."

So he looked and, amazingly enough, he couldn't find it either. "What address you lookin' for?"

I told him. "Four twenty-six North Park Drive."

"That's your problem then." He was being a good samaritan now. "This is South Park. Go outside and turn right and walk up about six blocks."

"Holy shit," I said. "You mean there's two parts to this street? Imagine that." And I walk out. I killed him four days later, but nowhere near North or South Park Drive.

So I waited for Squillante some more. He came out looking happy and content—and why shouldn't he, he had a nice afternoon while I was sitting there freezing—and drove back to his house. I almost dropped him there because I couldn't find a legal place to park. Most of the time I'll pull in next to a hydrant, but there was no way I wanted a cop to bother me while I was sitting on Squillante's block. All I need is a parking ticket putting me near his house a week before he's gunned.

I took one quick swing around the block and found a spot just beyond a bus stop, near a lamp post. By the time I parked he was out of the house and headed for the social club in the Tremont Avenue and Arthur Avenue area. This "social club" is nothing more than a big room on the bottom floor of a tenement-type building. I've never been inside this particular one, but if it's like all the others I've been in, it's got a pool table, some card tables, soda, candy and cigarette machines, a color television set, and a lot of chairs, usually filled with guys not doing too much of anything.

I don't know what Squillante was doing inside, but whatever it was didn't take him very long. He was out in ten minutes. I trailed him right back to his place and then said a fond adieu for the day. I had had enough of this bird.

And he still hadn't looked over his shoulder.

When I got home after bumping into Squillante I called Cockeyed Jimmy, as requested, and he told me the rest of my order had arrived. "Do me a favor, will ya, kid?" he asked. "Meet me at the trotters tomorrow night because I got a horse. Okay?"

Asking me to go to a race track is something like inviting a nympho to an orgy. There is absolutely no way in this entire world that I'm gonna turn down that invitation. I don't get that much opportunity to mix business with pleasure.

"You gotta promise me one thing, though," he added. "This horse goes in the sixth. No matter what I tell ya, don't give me my money before then because if you do I'll piss it away."

"You'd better be there on time then," I laughed, "because if you're not I'll piss it away for you."

Not only was he there on time, he was early. I met him just before the third race and he handed me a brown paper bag. I could feel the heavy metal silencer inside. I stuck the package in the pocket of my jacket and asked him, "You sure you don't want your money now?"

He was a changed man. He couldn't wait five minutes, much less until the sixth race. "Gimme my money. Gimme my money." The horses do that to people. So I handed him the money I owed him and, sure enough, by the time the sixth race came around he had pissed it away and he put the touch on me. It all worked out for the bettor, which was me, because the horse won and paid $46 and change. Those winnings paid for the gun and silencer.

One of my favorite comedians is a Hebe named Jackie Mason. He does this routine about guns. "Guns? Guns?" he says in a Jewish accent which I imitate very well. "Guns have never bothered me. I'm not at all scared of guns." Then he pauses and sticks his index finger in the air to make his point: "Bullets! Bullets are what bothers me."

My old lady is the same way. She knows it is necessary for me to keep guns around for business purposes, although she is not exactly sure what I use them for. She is smart enough never to ask me if I pull the trigger. But this lady is used to guns, and not afraid of them, and the only thing she ever asks me is not to leave guns lying around the house with bullets in them.

Guns are both my vocation and my avocation. A well-turned gun is really a piece of art and I have a couple of guns I will never use. I bought them and I keep them because I think they are beautiful. One is an authentic German Luger. The other is a specially made .38 automatic built on a .45 frame. This is one beautiful item.

Normally I do keep a few new guns lying around the house ready to be used if necessary. Plus I have the guns I carry when I'm conducting business of any kind. There are three of them. One is a regular .38 that I carry when I'm wearing heavy clothing in which it can easily be concealed. A second one is another .38 which I keep in the glove compartment of my car and the third isn't really a gun, it's more of a doomsday machine. It looks like a cigarette lighter, the same general size and shape, but in fact packs the punch of a small shotgun. I have specially made cartridges that screw into it. By pressing two little gold buttons I can blow away anybody within 30 feet.

I carry three guns for the same reason there are supposed to be three candles on a birthday cake. One for good luck. One for good health. And one to grow older with.

But I won't use any of these when I'm on a hit. I'll meet a supplier like Cockeyed Jimmy and place an order. The gun I get will be used only once and then it will be disposed of just as soon as safely possible. That doesn't mean I won't treat it just as well as any of the guns I use regularly. That gun is my job, my protection, my life. It is the whole ball game. If that gun lets you down when you need it, that is all she wrote, brother. So one of the most important things I have to do is prepare the gun and, eventually, test it.

After I left the track I went home for the first time that day. My wife had some fried chicken ready and after we finished eating we settled down to spend a quiet evening together. She curled herself up on the corner of the couch, her reading glasses half way down her nose, watching television and doing a needlepoint picture of a bunch of kittens trying to crawl out of a basket.

I started cleaning the gun I was going to kill Joe Squillante with. And most people say I don't strike them as the domestic type!

Since I work on my guns quite often, this was nothing unusual and my wife never said a word. As I said, as long as I don't load them in the house, she doesn't shoot off her mouth.

The gun was still wrapped, or rather had been rewrapped, in cosmoline oil and oilskin paper. I took a dry cloth and I wiped as much of the oil off as I possibly could. Then I wet the cloth and again wiped the gun down. That gets most of the oil, including the oil in the barrel, off the gun. Once I had gotten rid of as much oil as I thought I could get rid of, I took another dry cloth and went over the gun one more time. I went right through the whole thing, into the barrel, into the cylinders, down into the crook to where the hammer is, inside and outside until I had the whole thing shining.

Then I took my wife's sewing machine oil, which is a very light oil, and put just one drop down into the trigger housing to keep it lubricated. This is to prevent it from rusting on you and jamming when you don't want it to jam. I also put some oil on the cylinder so it would spin easily and another drop in the barrel, again to prevent rust. After that I just wrapped it up in a dry cloth and put it away in my drawer until I'm ready to test it.

I could tell the gun had been opened and then rewrapped because there was no serial number on it. The people I deal with are very careful people and they don't leave anything to chance. Not even me. To leave anything to chance is tantamount to suicide, so the serial number had been filed off. This is to protect the people who sold me the weapon more than to protect me. Without a serial number I have absolutely no way of finding out where the gun came from, if I wanted to, which I never do. The police don't have that problem. They can take a gun in a laboratory and somehow bring out the remnants of the number, even after it has been filed away.

But habit is a strange thing. Even knowing that the police could get the number, if the serial number had been on the gun I most probably would have filed it away with a grating file. However, if the serial number had been on the barrel, and many of them are, I wouldn't have even bothered because if you file away too much of the barrel it'll split open when you fire, and that is one opening I don't want to attend personally.

The whole operation, cleaning and oiling, took me maybe an hour and a half. This is one area in which time is not of the essence, but thoroughness most definitely is.

As I sat and cleaned my gun and my wife worked away at her needlepoint, we watched the television. I remember we had a "loud discussion" about what to watch at 10 P.M. I don't remember what she wanted to see, but I made my pitch for a police-detective program. I like those type shows because they always get their man, and I have always enjoyed fantasies. We flipped a coin and it turned out even—I got to watch what I wanted and she kept the coin.

It was a real homey scene, the little woman and her needlepoint, the hit man and his .38. It didn't last that long. It was only a little after 11 when I finished, but I had been up unusually early, there was nobody worth watching on the Carson show and I was tired. So I did something very extraordinary, I decided to pack it in for the night. My wife couldn't believe it. "What's the matter? You sick?" Some great sense of humor this woman has.

I picked up on Squillante at the coffee shop again Thursday morning. I just wanted to make sure there were no unusual breaks in his routine. Although it was still too early to start any real planning, I was thinking mainly about Hunts Point. I also decided I'd better take a more careful look at the Randall Avenue project just in case he decided to go there at night.

The chase had been smooth, but boring, and threatening to get even more boring. One of the things I really dislike about New York radio is that they decide a month before what the top 15 songs are going to be and play them to death. The same songs, over and over. Whenever I meet a disc jockey I expect he's going to say, "Hello, hello, hello, how, how, how, are, are, are" . . . and so on.

Squillante did not disappoint me. He made his two stops at the cab garages and his stop on the Grand Concourse and zipped right to the bank. Then back uptown and I thought he was going to his girlfriend's but he fooled me, he went home. I was sort of surprised, so I stayed with him and when he parked, I decided to wait him out. I had no idea what he was going to do so I sat there. And sat there. And sat there. And sat some more. Of all the things he could have done this afternoon, he did the one thing I didn't figure. Nothing. He stayed inside all fucking day. Seven and one-half hours.

A lot of things go through your mind as you sit there watching a door. You can't take your eyes off that door for one minute. You do and your chicken is liable to fly the coop. I've tailed guys and tailed guys, and I was either looking the other way or I was so punchy that my mind didn't register, but they've walked out and I've missed them. This is no big deal, you lose people all the time. In one case I had been sitting outside this hood's girlfriend's house all day and finally got out to take a piss and get some fresh air. I'm pissing and he's leaving. Only I don't know he's leaving.

So you try to concentrate all the time you're sitting

there watching nothing. Waiting for movement. And thinking. Sometimes thoughts you don't want come into your mind. When I'm alone like that, sitting, watching, waiting, the radio playing in the background, the thing I think mostly about is my first wife. I think about her quite a bit, as ridiculous as that sounds. I know I'm married to a good woman today, but this kid, my first wife, she is just something I never got out of my system. If you find a woman, a super-special woman, and she comes into your life, everything changes. And that is exactly what she was. I think if she had been alive I would never have gone into this business. Now, because she's dead, every single time I hit one of these guys I feel I just hit some more of the fucking scum that in one way or another was responsible for her death. This is the way I psych myself up.

I hadn't reached that point with Squillante yet, perhaps because I really knew him as a person, as a flesh-and-blood guy with a wife and a family, but I knew it would come. At this point I was mad at him for leading such a dull life. I had been sitting there almost five hours, nothing. In fact, I must have even gotten a little drowsy just staring at the door, because all of a sudden I hear a tapping at my window.

Shit, I thought before I turned around, I've attracted attention.

And I had. A little old lady who must have easily been in her 70s was tapping away. I opened my window, trying to keep an eye on the door as I talked to her. "Yeah?"

She must have had a lot of practice at being a busy-body, but she seemed really concerned. "Excuse me, but I was looking out my window . . . I live just across the street," she pointed right at Squillante's building, "and I could not help but notice you've been sitting here for a long time."

"Yeah, well," I interrupted, "you see, I've got to because . . ." Her ears perked up. "Because, you know." I stopped.

She didn't say anything. She just shook her head from side to side. Her way of telling me she didn't know.

"It's like this," I finally managed to respond. "My kids have this dog and it got away and we used to live here and . . . and the dog got used to that lamp post . . . over there . . . and I'm just sitting here waiting for the dog. There! That's why!" I considered that a marvelous story.

She was not quite convinced. "What kind of dog?" she questioned.

I said the first thing I could think of. "A Great Dane."

She obviously had heard of Great Danes. "Well, I'm Mrs. Gibson and I live in apartment 4G right across the street, and if you get cold you just come right in, mister . . . mister . . ." It was a question.

"Gold! Joey Gold!" It was an answer.

"Mr. Gold. Meanwhile I'll keep a watch out for your dog."

"You do that Mrs. Gibson."

"And where should I call you if I find him."

"Oh," I replied quite serious, "right here. I'll be right here every day until that dog is found. My children love him very much."

She was taken with me. "What a wonderful father. You know, Mr. Gibson would have been a wonderful father too, only we couldn't have any children."

"I'm sorry to hear that," I said, still watching the door.

"Yes," she said, "it was his war injury. He fought in World War One." I couldn't believe I was sitting here listening to some nutty grandmother tell me she couldn't have any children because of World War I. But I couldn't move. Finally she finished gabbing. "I must go now."

"I'm sorry," I said, but I didn't mean it.

"You're lucky Mr. Gold, you know that?"

I asked her why.

"You know there are all kinds of bad people in this city today. So when I see a car just sitting here for so long, like yours, sometimes I call the police." She now had my full, undivided attention.

"But you didn't this time, right?"

She knotted her brow. "Of course I did," she said flatly. I reached to start the engine to get away, but she continued. "But personally, between you and me, I think they're getting a little tired of hearing from me. They told me to come out and get the license plate of the car and call them back so they could check it from there."

I relaxed a bit. "But you're not going to do that now, are you Mrs. Gibson?" I asked.

She smiled. "Of course not. There's no need anymore, is there?"

I agreed completely. "No need at all," I said.

She trotted off to her window. I marked that up as an extra bit of luck. Some things you simply cannot plan for, and Mrs. Gibson was one of them. The trick is to survive them, as I had. Or at least as I thought I had.

Squillante hadn't moved yet. I spent another hour sitting there. I didn't play any mind games because I was afraid I would lose. But finally, just as I was beginning to think about leaving, out comes my man, dressed, to kill. He had put his whole seven thousand a week into this outfit. A beautiful formal suit with all the matching accessories. And he was alone.

There was no doubt in my mind where he was going: right back to Randall Avenue to pick up his broad for a night on the town. I could see myself sitting across the street from the Copa and probably a few other places and that did not appeal to me to any great extent. But Buster fooled me again. He went bing! Hopped in his car and drove directly to beautiful Brooklyn . . . to a wedding. I couldn't believe it was really a wedding so I stopped at a phone booth, called information and got the number of the place, and phoned. That is exactly what it was. Only friends of Squillante would get married on a Thursday night.

I figured they could get married without my standing guard, and I still had to get back uptown to my bookmaking office so I could settle with them for the week, so I kissed him goodbye.

After making my stop I drove home and got ready to make myself dinner. My old lady wasn't there and she didn't leave me anything to make, so I knew we would have some sort of argument when she came home. I don't mind if she goes out, as long as she leaves me something already prepared or something I can cook up myself. I hate driving around looking for a parking space and then have to turn around and go right out to get something to eat.

I was so pissed I drove all the way down to Chinatown for some Chinks. I started thinking along the way that I wasn't really so mad with my wife as I was with Squillante. This boy was making things too easy for me. I couldn't understand why a man doing the things he supposedly was doing wasn't being more careful. It bothered me. I wanted to see him look over his shoulder. I wanted him to be nervous, and he wasn't. And, more important, I wanted him to make some bets. One bet. Anything to let me know he is what he is supposed to be.

I got home about 11:30. My wife was there with some news. but before she gave it to me I started in on her. "What's the idea of going out and leaving nothing here?"

"What do you mean nothing? There was tuna fish, salami, bologna . . ."

"I don't mean crap. I mean food."

We were yelling at each other now. "What am I, your servant? I've got my own life to lead too, you know."

I started to interrupt, but she didn't let me. "Listen, I . . ."

"You never call and tell me where you are or when you're coming home. I don't know if you're going to be here for dinner, or not at all. So why should I bother? Huh? Tell me, why?"

It was obvious she had not had a good day. I figured I'd better soften her up. "Okay!" I screamed. Then I said it a little softer. "Okay, I'm sorry, you're right. I'm sorry."

We talked a little more, and made up. And then, as we were getting ready to go to bed, she dropped the bomb on me. "Guess who I called today?"

I couldn't guess.

"Cindy Squillante. I invited them over for dinner a week from Sunday."

YOUNG LADIES AND
OLD LADIES

On Friday I got very nervous.

Thursday night had been bad enough. My first reaction to my wife's news was to explode, but I caught myself in time. I wanted to tell her to cancel the invitation, but I had absolutely no reason to give her. It was much too far in advance to tell her I didn't feel like having company that night, and she wouldn't believe me if I told her that I didn't like Joe or Cindy Squillante. So I decided to let nature take its course. Perhaps with a little help from me. I knew there was every chance Squillante would not live long enough to share my roast beef.

On Friday morning I picked him up at the funeral home. I parked across the street waiting for him to come out, and as I did I watched a funeral. I never did like watching funerals or going to them.

I wondered what was going on inside, what Sweetlips was telling him. After all, the guy knew Squillante was just not going to show up one day. He didn't know when, I had no reason to tell him that, just one day there would be no Squillante and maybe a story in the *Daily News*. Jackie would have to pretend he was upset, but carry on and name a new controller. That's what he would have to do after. But this was before and I wondered if Jackie was surprised when Squillante showed up in the morning.

And then I thought of the other possibilities. That what they might be talking about in the funeral home was my funeral. Instinctively, I looked in my rearview mirror. All I saw was a hearse, which did nothing for my confidence. I would have given up the winner in a daily double to know what was going on inside.

When Squillante did come out, about a half-hour late, which bothered me, he got in his car and started driving back up to the Bronx. So far no problems, I'm just laying on his tail and watching him. He stopped at the social club for maybe an hour and played some cards and dicked around. Then he got back in his car and started driving back down toward Manhattan. I can't figure out where he's going, so I move in a little closer. This is an interesting new development.

He kept going right into Brooklyn and I cannot figure out where he's going at this time of day. As we were driving I checked my .38 to make sure it was loaded. Not that I was itchy. Maybe just a little itchy.

Then one of those bad things which sometimes happen happened. We ran into heavy traffic and he made a couple of lights that I caught, and he got waved through an intersection by a cop and I got caught, and before I knew it he was 15 blocks ahead of me and I'm losing him. I could see there was no way I was going to catch him on the avenue, so I figured I would make a right turn, parallel the avenue until I was ahead of him, and then make a left turn and get back on.

I did exactly that. I made my right, went about 30

blocks and then turned left back toward the avenue.
The traffic was as heavy as it had been before I turned
off—there must have been construction going on or an
accident, because there was no reason for this backup
as far as I could see—so I figured he had not reached
this point yet. I was in the middle of a pretty crowded
intersection, one which had rows of stores on both
sides of the street, so I pulled over to the curb in a bus
stop, to watch the passing traffic until he went by.

By the time I saw him, it was too late.

My timing had been very bad. Somewhere along the
line the traffic must have moved because he had beaten
me to the intersection and parked his car. He was on
foot and crossing the street directly in front of me. I
looked right at him and he looked right back at me. At
least I thought he looked at me, but he didn't register
any emotion. He just kept right on walking. He was
carrying a fur coat in his hand which answered my
question about why he had come to Brooklyn. But
that thought came later. For the moment I was
stunned. I didn't know if he had seen me or not.

I tried to figure. There were some very interesting,
and dangerous possibilities. If Squillante had indeed
seen me his first natural reaction should have been
to walk over to the car and say hello, how are you,
how's the old lady. The fact that he looked and kept
walking meant that either he didn't see me, maybe the
sun was glaring off the windshield or he wasn't paying
attention, or that he did and chose not to acknowledge
the fact.

It was the second possibility that bothered me. If he
did see me and pretended he didn't, there were only
two possible reasons. One: He made a quick and accurate deduction. He knew I killed people. Maybe he
never actually heard of a specific hit, but he knew.

Now, with what he was doing, the man had to be wary. In fact, one of the things that continued to bother me was his self-confidence. A man doing the things they said he was doing *should be nervous*. He wasn't. But if he was guilty, he probably expected to see me, or one of my co-workers, for a long time, and had been ready. So when he saw me parked in Brooklyn he didn't panic. He knew it was either a coincidence or he was being tailed. But he didn't panic. Or two: He knew I had been following him, *because he was told by Sweetlips*. And that this job was slowly being turned around on me. Simply by following Squillante, anyone who wanted to track me could do so. I would have to be on his tail. It was not a pleasant thought.

I turned the engine on and got out of Brooklyn just as fast as my Firestones would carry me. I had planned on stopping by to see this broad I know, but business before pleasure. I wanted to think this thing out. If he didn't see me I had no problems. If he did see me, and the deal was straight, he was either going to try to bluff it through or make a run for it. If the deal wasn't straight, he would act as if nothing had happened. I figured the time had come to pay a visit to Jackie Sweetlips at his used-car lot.

The place was on Jerome Avenue and he carried a lot of junk. He did pretty good but he could have done much better if he encouraged business. But what did he need it for? I walked into the small shack that served as his office and started to say hello. Before I got it out of my mouth, we were out of the place and standing in the open air.

"What'samatter?" I asked.

"The walls have ears," he said. He tried to act casual, but his tongue gave him away. He was not very happy to see me. "How's it going?"

"So far it's going," I said, acting casual and doing a better job of it than him. "Listen, I want to ask you a few questions. Is it possible he knows anything?"

Jackie shook his head. "No way. No way in the world. Number one, if he figured we were on to him the one place he wouldn't show up is the bank, and he ain't missed yet. Number two, he's planning another heist for next week. One of his hoods called me this morning and asked me what to do."

"And what's to do?"

"I told him I'd get back to him. I wanted to speak to you first. When do you think Squillante will be grounded?"

I paused. I was the one trying to get information. I didn't want Jackie to know what my plans were. "Who knows. I'll know pretty well by Monday."

He made a minor attempt to apologize for rushing me. "It's no problem either way. We can set up the heist or tell the punk to put him off another week. No big deal."

We both knew it was. Eventually Squillante would have to get suspicious if his men keep putting him off. I leaned on a 1963 Chevy that was so covered with dirt and dust some P.R. named "Ricardo" had scrawled his name on the hood. I brushed the dirt off my jacket. "How do you expect to sell cars when they're so dirty?"

He watched me brush the dirt off. "Send me the cleaning bill."

"Don't laugh," I said, "I will." Then I decided to ask him about the morning. "Hey, I picked him up at the bank this morning and he was more than a half-hour late leaving. How come?"

"We were putting on a show for him," Jackie said very matter-of-factly and very believably. "We don't want any of the controllers to know we grabbed the stick-up boys so every now and then we hold one of them after work and pump them for information. Today was Squillante's turn."

"And?"

"He didn't know a thing."

"Imagine that," I answered, trying to make a joke. The story was certainly logical enough. I just didn't know if it was true or not. I paused for a minute. If I was the center of Sweetlips's attention I didn't want him to know that I suspected it. I decided to gamble. "Hey, Jackie, why me?"

"Whattya mean?"

"I mean, you and I don't get along so good, that's a known fact. So how come the Fat Man picks me?"

Now it was Jackie's turn to pause. I watched for the tongue, but it didn't show. Either he was telling the truth or he had practiced this conversation before. "Don't ask me," he answered. "I just follow orders. We had a meeting and Petey suggested you and . . ."

"What'd you do when Petey said me?"

"I'll be honest wit' ya. I didn't want you. I wanted somebody else. But the Fat Man ain't got no love for my suggestion. He knows your rep and he didn't want no foul-ups. So he said it was you. Like I said, I only do what the man tells me."

"Well, then. How do you feel about it?"

He looked me right in the eye. Then he spit on the ground. It was a very honest answer.

"Glad we're clear about that," I said. "Okay, I'll let you get back to washing these lemons. I'll see you around." We both turned and started walking our separate ways, me back to my car and Jackie back into the shack. But there was one more question I wanted to ask him. I knew I wouldn't be able to depend on the answer, but deep in the back of my mind there was another possibility developing. Maybe there was no plot aimed at me, maybe the whole thing was legitimate. And maybe they simply had the wrong guy. "Hey, Sweetlips." I stopped him in his tracks. He turned and looked at me. "Are you people sure he's the right guy?"

He looked disgusted, like he had been through this too many times and now it was beginning to become a pain in his neck. "Ain't you seen him betting?"

"Not yet," I lifted my voice across the lot. "Not one goddam time."

"Don't worry about it, kid," he said. "He's the one. You let us take that responsibility." He went back inside.

Jackie made me feel no better. I was beginning to realize that I wouldn't really know for sure what was going on until the final confrontation. If then. I resolved to make sure that I was the one who had all the advantages when it came.

I started to drive back toward Squillante's place after leaving the lot, but then I decided to leave him alone for a while. I didn't want to take the chance of having him see me twice in one day, assuming he did see me in Brooklyn. That would have tied it from his point of view. So instead I decided to go see Alice-with-the-big-tits.

Alice lived in the Chelsea section of Manhattan, on West 16th Street between Seventh and Eighth Avenues. This was fine because it was far, far away from places where people knew me. I may play around a little, but I don't want my wife knowing about it no how. My wife has been too good to me to embarrass her by throwing some other broad in her face, so when I do play I do it very quietly and very discreetly.

By this time I had been seeing Alice about five months. Originally I met her through a betting customer of mine. Whenever I saw him, she would be with him. I thought she was a cute kid with an exceptional body. One day I went over to see him and she wasn't there. Turns out they had broken up a month earlier. "What kind of broad is she?" I asked him.

"She's a good lady."

"Gimme her number," I told him and he did. I gave her a call and we started going out. It was a nice thing. She worked, when she worked, for a temporary agency. And sometimes, when she wasn't working regularly, I would help her out with a few dollars. It was nice, it was convenient, it was satisfying.

I would see her at least once a week, but rarely more than twice a week. The only rule I made was that I would never see her too often on the same day of the week. You can never tell when somebody is tracking you. I had called her Thursday night and told her I'd be there by 1:30. Because of Squillante it was after 3 P.M. when I arrived.

"You're late," she said as I walked in. "I've been expecting you for two hours." She was dressed in a pretty short skirt and a pretty tight sweater. Tight sweaters really did something for her. They also did something for me. She knew her tits were spectacular and did everything she could to emphasize them. As I said, a smart girl. Besides her body, the thing I liked best about her was the fact that she never wore any underwear when I came to visit. Just knowing there was nothing but flesh under that skirt and sweater made my blood boil.

"Business," I told her and then I grabbed her. She

knew that I was in the rackets but she never knew that I used a gun, although I'm sure she liked to imagine that I did, and this turned her on. I wasn't in any mood for small talk or formalities. I just wanted to fuck. She didn't care at all. Alice liked sex just as much as I did. She liked to be handled roughly which is why I think she went for me. I was good at that. I never would hurt her—I've never hurt a woman in my life—but I'd put on the big tough-guy act and half rip her clothes off.

I spent the whole afternoon fucking Alice and forgetting about Squillante. Both with great success. I wasn't going home for dinner, so we called Chicken Delight and had them deliver. By the time we got through screwing and eating it was after seven o'clock. I gave her a greasy kiss and went on my way.

I started to drive home and then I changed my mind and turned to go toward a social club to play some cards. Before I went six blocks I changed my mind again and decided to find an empty alley and bowl a few games and think. That decision didn't last long. I finally decided to drive past Squillante's place and see if everything looked all right. I wasn't worried about him seeing me at night. Even with the best lights it's very difficult to see inside a moving car after dark.

His car was parked outside and everything looked exactly as it should. By that I mean a light was on. I parked in my usual spot, near the lamp post, planning to stay a few minutes just to see if maybe I could catch a lucky break. I'm not sure what I was looking for, some sign, some signal, that he hadn't noticed me. There was nothing. I sat there about a half-hour and then the front door opened.

Walking right toward me was Mrs. Gibson.

I had no choice but to open my window.

"I saw you pull up and I thought maybe you'd like some coffee."

"Oh, how nice," I replied, "but I must be leaving soon. So I can't come in."

Her face puckered up. "Oh, no," she said. "I brought it out for you." And she held up a thermos jar. Before I could say another word she poured me a cup of coffee. "Do you like cream and sugar?"

I allowed that I did.

She reached into one pocket and pulled out a container of cream. She pulled two sugar cubes out of her other pocket. The woman was a walking supermarket. As she mixed she told me another bit of thrilling news. "I've put signs up all over the building for you. If anyone finds the dog I told them to call me."

I managed to show enthusiasm. "That's wonderful Mrs. Gibson," I told her. "How thoughtful of you." I sat there drinking my coffee talking about Great Danes to this old bat, and thinking about the problem she was causing. For all I knew she could have been the Squillantes' next door neighbor, maybe even their babysitter. Who knew what she was saying to anybody, how she was describing me, and how often? She certainly could describe me. When she stuck her puss in the car she was no more than six inches away.

And after the hit, would she think to tell the coppers about "that nice Mr. Gold," who spent hours sitting outside her building, "the same building in which that nice Mr. Squillante used to live?" That could cause me great heartache.

There was nothing I could do about it though, except be nice to the old bat. My business was fulfilling contracts, not blasting little old ladies. I've never killed an innocent person in my life. But, and this is an important but, if an innocent person saw me make a hit I'd have to seriously consider it. Thus far it has never happened to me. It has happened to other people though. In one case a hood brought his perfectly pure girlfriend to a "business meeting," which was actually a setup. They both went. In another recent case out on Long Island this model was called to testify about her boyfriend. They found her floating in Long Island Sound. It happens.

I finished my coffee. "Listen, Mrs. Gibson, I've got to get home to my family. The little woman and the little children." I really poured it on. She loved every minute of it.

Squillante never showed his face.

I went home and spent a very restless night.

Saturday is no different than the rest of the week for a numbers runner. He's got to be up and at work just as early as the other days to see his people. Bettors don't know a five-day week and when they want to bet you'd better be around to take their money or they'll find someone else to give it to. Squillante left his house right on time. I was there waiting for him.

I was ready for him to start making strange turns to see if he was being followed—if that started, I would just drop him for the day. But he gave no indication of being any more worried or nervous than he had been all week. And that was not at all.

It is an interesting thing about being tailed. If you think you are being followed it is very easy to check it out. All you have to do is make four right turns in a row, or go right, left, right, left or some combination with no meaning to it, and if one car keeps following you then you've got a partner. But if you don't know you're being watched it's difficult to pick up on it. I've been trailed a number of times, and I've almost never managed to pick up on it. It almost got me killed a few times.

I was working for Meyer Lansky at the time doing a little of this and a little of that, mostly being a bodyguard. Some people wanted to get rid of him and tried to get me to go along. When I refused they decided to eliminate me. Normally I'm not a nervous person, but I do look, I do check, whenever I get that itchy feeling. I had it this time but it did me no good, I couldn't pick them out. I never had the slightest idea they were on me.

They picked the perfect location. I had a heavy coat on and was walking out of the bank after picking up a payroll for Meyer. There were 9000 people standing around who started to panic when they saw guns, and I wasn't ready for my friends. They also did it in the middle of the rush hour when no cop in the world could get through the traffic.

They air-conditioned my body a bit, but they didn't kill me. I killed two of them in the attempt, and Meyer sent me to Brazil to recover.

I was also followed in Reno, Nevada, when my first wife was killed. These three guys could have killed me easily, but instead they tried to break my head open with a lead pipe. They put me in a hospital 15 months, but they didn't kill me. Again, I didn't have the slightest idea I was being tailed.

One time I did realize I had company was when a couple of amateurs tried to make some extra cash. My old lady and I went to the theater and dinner in Manhattan. I had parked the car on 48th Street between Ninth and Tenth because I wasn't going to spend five dollars to put it in a lot for a few hours. We were walking toward the car and I looked behind me, I always look over my shoulder when I walk down dark streets, and this time there were two niggers walking slowly behind us. Oh, can you imagine that, I said to myself. I just knew they were going to try to rip me off, there was absolutely no doubt about that in my mind.

"Just keep walking," I told my wife, "and don't say a word." She did just exactly like I said. I had my piece on me and I pulled it out and covered it with my hand. I let my wife move ahead and about 30 yards from the car these guys started running and caught up to me. I turned around and one of them has a long, thin blade out. "Gimme your money, man," he ordered.

I laughed right in his face. "How do you want it, man," I said, imitating the way he said "man." I showed them the piece. "In the head or in the belly?" I put the duo against a building and proceeded to rob them. One of them had $250 and the other had $300. The first one had a nice diamond ring, the other a beautiful gold bracelet made of $20 gold pieces. These gentlemen had obviously been very successful in their previous endeavors. I took it all.

The guy who had the knife finally complained. "Hey, man, what you rippin' us off for? We work the same side of the street."

"No way fuckface," I told him, "no way." I told them to walk the other way and when they reached the end of the street I got in my car and drove away. I handed my wife most of the money. "Here honey," I told her, "you just got yourself a surprise present for doing just like I told you to."

So I've picked up maybe one tail out of three at least, which means I'm hitting .333, though I admit my one hit was off amateur pitching. Squillante's average was either .1000 or .000. I would not know for a while yet.

He spent Saturday acting like he didn't have a care in the world. My only question was whether it was just an act. I didn't believe he could possibly be that stupid, intentionally. He had to be worried and he wasn't. So I worried for him.

He went where he was supposed to. He went to the projects, the street corners, the cab garages. He met all the people he was supposed to meet and made all his pickups. He went to the bank and dropped off his proceeds. He made his last few pickups and returned to the bank. And then, his day's work done, he went directly to his girlfriend's for an afternoon's entertainment. I settled down for a long winter's stay. It could have been worse, there were some very decent college football games on the radio and I didn't have to listen to no music at all.

One of the things I do when I'm sitting and waiting is time the police patrols, particularly if the area is a potential hit spot. Sometimes they're irregular and you can't get any schedule. That alone can make a location doubtful. The one thing you don't want is a patrol car riding in on you when you're sitting there with a loaded gun waiting for the intended.

The Randall Avenue project had a few things to recommend it, but it was not a first choice. I figured though, as long as I was sitting there, I might as well get a line on the cops. The first car came by 20 minutes after I parked. This gave me a starting place. The same car reappeared 45 minutes later, and 45 minutes or so after that. Meanwhile, Squillante was still inside, pumping away at his Puerto Rican piece. Or so I assumed.

I really couldn't figure why Squillante would waste

his time with some spic when he had a broad like Cindy waiting for him at home. If I had a broad like that, I started thinking, and then figured why not? As soon as Squillante was dead and in the ground, I'd give her a call as any old and dear friend would, and maybe I would get her away for a few hours to help her forget, and then maybe I'd take her home and ball the daylights out of her.

Somebody was going to. She was young, pretty and very sexy. She wasn't going to become a nun. Somebody was going to get in her pants. Why not me? I seriously thought about it sitting there. I could almost see me and her sprawled across her bed, her nice, thin legs up in the air as I pumped away at her.

So, I thought, let Joseph Squillante have his Puerto Rican senorita. What I had waiting for me was a lot better. And to get at it, all I had to do was bury Squillante, my job.

I caught myself right there. When you start thinking like that, you get careless. Killing is not a crime of passion, it's a job. When you do it for love you get caught. I did it for money. And I didn't want to get the two mixed up.

Maybe, I thought, after he's been dead a few months. Maybe.

When the time came for the police car to come around again I got out of my car and walked down the block. I didn't know if they had noticed me or not, but I figured what the hell, I needed the air anyway. And I didn't need them checking to see what I was doing sitting there for three hours.

That walk proved to be a mistake on my part. In the few seconds it took me to get out of my car and walk down the block I missed Squillante's exit. Either that or he walked out the back door, or I missed him when I was thinking about balling his wife. I didn't know. In fact, I didn't know he left. After the patrol car came and went I resumed waiting in my car. Nothing happened for another 45 minutes, and again I took my walk. It's possible Squillante left at this point, I will never really know. By the time another three-quarters of an hour passed it was dark enough for me to stay in my car and not worry about patrols. Besides, I knew that they must have changed shifts somewhere along the line and two new patrolmen were riding the area.

In all I waited about six hours and nothing happened. Then the front door of the building opened and this good-looking chick walked out. I had never seen Squillante's broad before but I had a very bad feeling this was her. She looked exactly like the girlfriend described in Jackie's letter: small, long hair (the information sheet said it was reddish but I couldn't tell in the light), great figure and, this was the clincher, this broad was wearing the coat I saw Squillante carrying in Brooklyn. The coat was the thing that caught my attention. It was too good for any dame living in this particular project.

I was stunned. If Squillante was gone the only conclusion I could reach was that he was onto me. I turned my engine on and drove around the corner to check his car. Normally I never watch an individual's car, I watch the individual. One of the things I learned early in this business is that you never track a person by watching his transportation because he is liable to use several different kinds, particularly if he suspects he is being followed. It is an old law the army taught me: Never make an assumption. Deal with facts. With known things. In this case though I had to throw that law out: His car was gone. I made an assumption and it was very, very bad.

If he had skipped, no physical harm would come to me. Nobody is going to kill me if I blow the job and the man submerges. But it isn't going to help my reputation and I'm not going to be working too often for a while.

I couldn't spend time debating the facts. I had to move. I knew he was gone. What I didn't know was if he had given me the slip intentionally or if I had just missed him one time when I turned my head or walked down the block. If he had given me the slip intentionally that meant he knew somebody was on his ass. I had to find out in a hurry.

I drove my car around the block just in time to see this broad getting into a taxi. If he *had* given me the slip she was being awfully stupid by leaving the apartment. If I hadn't seen her I would have simply figured he was still up there doing whatever. I had a quick decision to make: Should I follow the cab or go to the one place I was usually pretty sure of picking him up at, his home? I started to follow the cab. If it had gone downtown, toward the airports, I would have followed it all the way. Instead she headed toward Westchester. I decided to take a gamble and I started driving like a madman toward Pelham Bay.

Every single person in the entire world has at least one place where they invariably show up. Everyone. Once, for example, I was looking for a guy and the only place I knew for sure I could find him was at the race track. The animals were running at Saratoga, but that's a goodly trip from New York City. I didn't think he would make the trek so, if he was going to the flats, he had to go to Monmouth Park. I went to Monmouth Park every day for 12 consecutive days to look for this guy and, sure as shit, on the 12th day this guy comes along. It cost me some money, as long as I was at the track I figured I might as well make a bet or two, but I found him.

In Squillante's case there were a number of places I could depend on finding him: his home, the numbers bank, his girlfriend's. I knew he wasn't at his girlfriend's. There was just no reason in the world he would go to the bank at this hour. That left his home.

He wasn't there. No car. Lights on in the living room. I drove around the block three or four times looking for his transportation. It just wasn't there. I was trying hard to relax but there was sweat on my face. Usually I can handle anything that comes along, but I don't make that many mistakes so I can get used to it. When I blow one it eats me up inside.

I tried to put myself in his place. If someone were after me, where would I run? Where would I hide? Car? Plane? Train? Maybe even a Greyhound? There were just too many options. The first thing I decided to do was call Sweetlips and have him put out the word that anyone seeing Squillante should contact him immediately. It was something I hated to do because it was an admission of failure, and I'm not good at admitting that, but it was something I had to do because I couldn't let him get too big a head start.

I started driving down the block toward a shopping center where I figured I could find a phone. And then I saw this beautiful sight. Joseph Squillante driving down the street from the opposite direction.

As he drove by I turned my head away and kept going straight. I made the first turn I could and zoomed back toward his place. I got there just in time to see him climbing out of his car with all sorts of packages. That son of a bitch had been shopping! I could have kissed him. He picked up his packages and walked inside. He didn't even look around. I'm clean, I thought. I'm clean.

I went right straight home and had a big, relaxing, restful, delicious dinner, prepared by my charming wife.

And I never even knew I had been tailed from the moment I left Randall Avenue.

SQUILLANTE
BETS HIS LIFE

So far the Squillante job had more problems than it was worth. Between wondering if Squillante was the guilty party, or if the thing was planned just to set me up, and now, if he had seen me, my concentration was shot to shit. All the time I spent wondering I should have been working out a plan. I had been on Squillante almost a full business week and still hadn't picked out a prime location. Usually I do that in the first few days, yet here I was still wavering between a number of places, really thrilled by none of them. Worse, in my own mind, I still had not resolved the two problems.

If Squillante was betting heavily he was doing it very quietly. All the time I had been with him I hadn't seen him pick up a racing form or go anywhere near the track. He might have been betting from his girlfriend's or even from his own living room, but that I doubted. He wouldn't have bet without studying the sheets and I never saw him buy one. And his betting was the key. If I could catch him getting down I would know for sure that he was the right target. And that I wasn't.

On Saturday night I decided to find out once and for all.

I called a friend of mine named Reg who is a phone mechanic. This means he can do anything that can be done with telephones, from running a backstrap for a bookie operation—that is two phones in two different locations hooked together on one number—to putting in a Princess phone with a lighted dial and low ring for my wife.

We exchanged pleasantries. "Whattya doing tomorrow morning?" I asked.

"I'm going to church. What do you think I do on Sunday mornings?"

I know Reg well enough to know that he hasn't been to church since the last Monte Carlo night. "You're probably sleeping in, you fucking lazy bum."

He sighed. "Do me a favor? Don't tell God."

"Don't worry," I laughed, "we ain't on speaking terms. Anyway I got my own problems. How'd you like to make a hundred bucks?"

"That's what I been praying for."

"Fine. I need some of your expert help. Bring your telephone tools and meet me outside Johnny Dee's place at eleven o'clock tomorrow morning."

"Whattya need?"

I don't like to discuss my business on the telephone under any circumstances. There was no way I was going to tell him now, particularly when I considered him to be the F.B.I. (finest bugging individual) I've ever known. "I want to tap a confessional," I told him. "I think I got a line on some priest trying to pass saltines off as wafers. What the fuck difference does it make why I want you there, just be there."

"What kind of place is it?" he asked in his best professional tone.

I told him, "An apartment house."

There was a short pause while he considered the job. "Alright," he finally agreed, "but I want to be home in time for the football game."

"You'll be home for the kickoff," I lied.

I picked him up in front of Johnny Dee's because I didn't want him to know where we were going. Reg is a Manhattanite and knows the Bronx like I know Buckingham Palace. At best he's heard of it. As long as I was driving I knew he would never remember where we were going. He had his tools in one hand and the *New York Times* in the other. "What's the newspaper for?" I asked him.

"To read," he said simply. You ask a stupid question . . .

I realized I was taking a big gamble going into Squillante's building, but I knew the odds against Squillante coming down into the basement on a Sunday morning were about the same as Francis the Talking Mule winning the Kentucky Derby. And if anyone else came down, Reg was carrying more telephone company identification than Alexander Graham Bell himself. Besides, this was a case where the ends justified any means. I simply had to find out.

We had absolutely no problem walking in the back entrance and going down into the cellar. Just to be on the safe side though, Reg thoughtfully gave me a telephone company hardhat to wear.

Reg found the terminal box immediately. The box itself was approximately 12 inches high and 8 inches wide. It opened up to reveal at least 25 different wires in a multitude of colors. "Which apartment does this guy live in?" Reg asked.

I told him and he began searching through the wires. Finally he found what he was looking for and he took two metal clips and hooked them onto the wire. Then he hooked the other end of the wires into a pair of earphones and handed them to me. I put them on and heard a dial tone.

"That's the apartment." I always thought Reg was wasting his time working for people in the organization. With talent like his he definitely should have been in politics.

I leaned against the wall and waited for something to happen. Reg sat down next to me and picked up the *Times*. He pointed at the paper and mouthed the words, "To read," and began doing so. Sometimes you get a stupid answer twice.

We were sitting down there for maybe a half-hour with absolutely no action. Then someone picked up the phone. Here we go, I thought, he's going to call his bookie and get down on some gridiron classics.

It was Cindy Squillante. She called some other woman and they gabbed a few minutes and then she invited this other broad and her husband for dinner during the week. Sure, I thought, them she invites over, but us she has to come to our place. We'll see about that! They kept talking.

Reg pointed to his watch. It was 70 minutes to kick-off time. The pregame show would be going on the air shortly. Get off the damn phone, I thought, get off the damn phone. Eventually they did, but before they finished I picked up a new recipe for chocolate icing.

Nothing happened for another 10 or 15 minutes. Reg was through with the sports and entertainment section and was deep into the book reviews when the phone rang. No matter how much he bet no bookie was going to call him to solicit his action. It was a wrong number. The earphones were hurting my ears and I took them off. "Hey Reg, is it possible they have two phones?"

He turned around and very quickly checked the box. I figured that was the problem, we had the wrong phone. While Squillante must have been busy betting, I was getting a chocolate icing recipe. Reg turned around. "One phone." He resumed his reading.

The time shot by and I was really getting uptight. If the man does not bet horses then he is betting football or he is simply not betting. That's it. And so far Squillante was not betting. It was one-half hour to kickoff.

Fifteen minutes later someone picked up the telephone. I recognized Squillante's voice. This was the call I was waiting for.

He starts betting football and I mean really betting. He makes six games, $5000 a game. Then he hangs up and calls another bookie and goes through the same routine again, this time at $2500 per game. This is my answer. This is where his money is going. I could not believe my ears. I was stunned. This stupid motherfucker was getting himself buried even worse than he had been. It really fractured me. He was on the boards for $45,000 and who knew how long it had been going on.

The bookies obviously let him go because they knew he was a good earner, and when you're earning they don't care how deeply you go into the hole. As long as he kept handing in $2000 a week or so I'd let him keep betting too. The odds are that he is never going to get even. You know what it takes to get out when you're down to something reasonable, even

$50,000? I own you, don't I? And as long as I know you're capable of earning I'll let you go on forever. Very rarely is an individual who is consistently making payments shut down even though he has no hope of ever getting even: It's when he starts missing payments that he is cut off. The one thing bookies don't want to do is make desperadoes out of their customers. Squillante had become a desperado.

I didn't have to hear any more. I don't even know if he made any more phone calls. People like him will start making cover bets at halftime, trying to win both halves of a game or at least break even. Sometimes they just go deeper in the hole. I tapped Reg on the shoulder and nodded. "I got him," I said, "let's go."

He carefully folded up his *New York Times,* took the clips off the wires and wrapped up his equipment. I drove him back to Johnny's place, pulled out my wallet and peeled off two hundred-dollar bills. I handed them both to him. "Thank you doctor," I told him. I could depend on Reg to keep his mouth shut simply out of friendship, but with friendship and money I knew I could depend a little more.

Neither me nor Reg got home in time for kickoff, but I got back in plenty of time to get down on some of the games outside the Eastern Standard Time Zone. Then I sat and watched the television action. I'm sure my old friend Squillante was doing exactly the same thing. And sweating.

I broke about even for the day but Squillante did not do so well. He got what we in the organization call buried. He lost five games and won one. Assuming he didn't make any more bets than those I heard, and that is an unlikely assumption, he dropped $33,750 for the day. This is because each $5000 bet came to $5500 and each $2500 bet was really $2750 when you add in the 10 percent vig, or service charge, that bookies include. His total winnings for the day were $7,500 and his losings were $41,500, a total of $33,750 in the hole. This is not chopped liver.

I took my wife to Chinatown for dinner that night, but my mind was not on chop suey. I focused squarely on Joseph Squillante. One of the problems had been answered: He was indeed the heavy bettor Sweetlips told me about. I began to feel a little safer knowing he was a legitimate target. But I was gonna keep checking my rear-view mirror.

One thing I do remember about this particular evening in Chinatown was the fortune I got in my cookie. In fact, I saved it and carry it in my wallet because it was so unusual, so silly and so accurate at the same time. "Do not make any decisions until you are quite certain."

Now I was quite certain. And I had made my decision.

Monday I decided to go through the whole morning thing with him one more time just to make sure he hadn't made any changes, and to make sure I hadn't overlooked any potential spots. I packed my pen, notepad, maps, portable radio, army blanket and wristwatch in my car and waited for him to get started. He came out a few minutes late and gunned the Buick trying to make up for lost time.

Nothing changed at all. He went from the restaurant at the end of Westchester Avenue to the coffee shop without missing a beat. He made all his stops, met all his runners, collected his due, and made up for the lost few minutes.

Once again I wasted a half hour sitting outside the coffee shop watching him warm up. I began to wonder strange things about Squillante. Like, how come he

drinks so much coffee and never seems to go to the
bathroom? I sniff the stuff and I'm pissing for half an
hour. Or, with all the money he had, how come he was
living in a small apartment? Or would his Puerto
Rican broad know what happened when he stopped
showing up? Or how pissed are his bookies going to
be when they read about his untimely end in the *Daily
News?* With such wonderful thoughts I passed the
waiting time.

He left the restaurant and hit the funeral-home
bank for awhile. From there back up to the cab garages on Jackson Avenue and then on to the Grand
Concourse. Zoom—back to the bank and right on
time. Finished for the day.

While I was waiting for him I made myself a list of
places he might head for. But he fooled me again, he
went to a beauty parlor.

It was just another strange twist I couldn't figure
out. He drove directly from the bank down into Lower
Manhattan and he stopped in front of a beauty parlor
on Eighth Avenue in the 20s. He walked right in. I've
had guys go to all sorts of places on me. Real rank
whorehouses, baseball games, deserted warehouses,
bus depots, VFW meetings. I even had a guy go to a
queer bar once, which really threw me, especially
when he came out with another guy, but I have never
had a guy go to a beauty parlor on me before.

At first I figured this must be one of the places that
were just opening up around that time that catered to
men and women. In fact, two guys went into the place
a little after Squillante arrived, but no more. And there
was no sign outside to indicate that men were wel-
come. I was curious, but I didn't really try to guess.
There was no reason to. I knew the fact: He went

there. He was in there almost an hour and he came out looking no prettier than he did when he went in.

Something that doesn't happen that often was starting to happen: I was picking up more than Squillante's movements; I was picking up his rhythm. There is really no way to explain exactly what I mean by that. It was just that I was beginning to feel in tune with his movements. We were together. I *knew* his physical movements, but somehow I was feeling his mental movements. This is an intangible that I never get on most hits. Usually it's just trace, track and shoot. This wasn't true with Squillante. We were operating on the same tracks, but going in opposite directions. Of course, only one of us knew there was going to be a collision. At least, that's what I believed.

From the beauty parlor he went back up to the Bronx and right to the social club on Arthur Avenue. He usually locked his car only when he was going to be parked for awhile. When he stopped at the social club he locked the Buick. He was here to stay. I settled back and turned on the portable radio.

Squillante must have been playing cards in the club because he did not come out until later in the afternoon. And he did not come out alone, which in itself did not surprise me. I didn't know the guy he was with but it's not unusual for one individual to give a lift home to another individual so I didn't give it a thought. They were in a deep discussion and Squillante's friend was waving his arms and gabbing away a mile a minute. For a few seconds he looked so angry I thought he might pull a piece and do my job for me. But eventually they both were laughing and got into Squillante's car. I started following.

We headed uptown, toward the Bronx. I hadn't been checking to see if I was being followed, as I promised myself I would. Now, with nothing else to do except listen to the "number seven hit in New York land!" I started paying attention to what was behind me.

And I got very itchy. A 1965 Chevy sedan with two men in it was about four car lengths behind me. Nothing unusual about that. But when I speeded up they speeded up, they stayed four car lengths behind me. Nothing particularly unusual about that. And when I moved from the left lane into the center lane, they too moved over one lane. Nothing particularly unusual about that. Finally I put my blinker on, like I was getting off at the next exit, and moved over to the right lane. Their blinker went on. Nothing particularly unusual about that. But when the exit came I sailed right past it.

They did too! Now I've found something unusual. I'm beginning to believe I got myself some partners.

I dropped Squillante at the next exit and got off. The Chevy sedan followed. I drove a few blocks straight ahead and started making turns. The car followed for the first four, then dropped off. If they were trailing me, and I was sure they were, they must have realized I picked them up. In a way I was sorry about that. I would have liked to get close enough to see who these people were. I might have recognized one of them.

I pulled over to the side and waited. I watched the rear-view mirror and looked straight ahead, seeing if they were trying to circle around and pick me up again. I waited 20 minutes but they never reappeared. It didn't make any difference. Someone was trailing me. The only question was who.

I figured two possible choices. Maybe old Joe Squillante was not as stupid as he seemed to be. Perhaps the reason he wasn't looking over his shoulder was that he didn't have to—he had some people doing the looking for him. Or maybe Jackie Sweetlips is taking advantage of a good situation and making it better—for himself. I was going to burn Squillante, as instructed by the Fat Man, and then Jackie was going to burn me.

Neither possibility filled me with great joy.

If the tail was sponsored by Squillante, then the hit was in jeopardy. If his boys had been tailing me long enough to see that I was following him, my cover was blown. He would have no doubts about what a tail meant, and he would either have to fight or run, and do it quickly.

If the tail came from Sweetlips the problem would not be as great. I doubt he would give me credit for being smart enough to realize he set it up. But he certainly would be more careful in the future.

There was nothing more I could do about it at this point anyway. I closed my notepad for the day and went home.

By the time I found a place to park, checked to see that no one had followed me home, and walked over to my building, it was past seven o'clock. I figured I would call the office and see how we did, then stay home all night and read my notes. The time had come for me to start making some serious decisions about Squillante's future, or lack of same. It was going to be a quiet, thoughtful night at the old Joey apartment.

Wrong! Usually I have a pretty good memory for things my wife tells me, but I was surprised to hear a lot of noise when I opened my front door. It took me a second, then I realized this was the girls' night at my place. Each Monday night my wife meets these five ladies at one of their places and they play canasta or poker or Mah-jongg or go to a movie or just gossip. This week it was my lucky turn. This was exactly what I needed. I've got to sit down and plan a murder and these girls are busy driving me insane.

I'm never sure if they're glad to see me or not. They know I'm in the business but they don't know exactly what I do. Sometimes I like to put on a tough-guy act for them, I overdo it on purpose, which they seem to love. We get along all right. Whenever I get some panty hose or some double-knits I'll give them first shot. And whenever I'm sending a truck down for some cigarettes I let them know about it and they spread the word at their offices or to their friends. Between the five of them they can usually get rid of anywhere between 250 and 500 cartons.

"Who wants cigarettes?" I asked as I sat down and grabbed some of the cold chicken my old lady was feeding them. With the exception of Phyllis, whose husband is a dentist and who refuses to buy from me because she believes she is financing organized crime and therefore paying for every possible evil, they started screaming and shouting. I assume they were making a couple of dollars on cigarettes for themselves and I didn't care. I told them to call my wife before Friday and give her their orders.

I was deep into a chicken leg when Patti, who looks like an opera singer and has a high, squeaky voice that just irritates the hell out of me, demanded, "Have you got anything else?"

"What do I look like, a goddam department store?" They all laughed. I had to be a little careful in front of these ladies because my wife doesn't like me to curse. But they loved the whole act. Their husbands were just normal husbands. Patti's husband ran a drug store. Diane's was a mailman and I don't know what Barbara's or Betty's husbands did. But for the ladies I was better than going to the movies, I was the "real thing." "Yeah, I got sumthin' else," I told them, in dialect. "I got me twenty reel sets of skin flicks. I can let you have them for seven dollars apiece or a hundred for the whole set. Who wants a set?" They laughed some more. Actually I did have access to the movies but none of the girls wanted any. Besides, my old lady would have killed me.

I finished my chicken and got up to retire to the bedroom. "Where're you going?" my old lady asked.

"I got to go inside and plan a killing," I said in a loud voice. The girls loved it, and went back to their playing and dining.

Actually what I did first was find out whether I was rich or poor. There had been a number of point upsets in the pro games Sunday—most of the favorites won but only a few covered the point spread—so I didn't figure we had done too badly. The office confirmed my beliefs, we were in the black by approximately $7500. For me $7500 is a big week because I don't have many very big bettors. Nobody like Squillante, for example. I don't need them or want them because eventually they're going to either break you or you'll break them. It's the inevitable result. I wrote down my winners and losers and set aside a good portion of Tuesday to settle up.

I started to take out my notes on Squillante but I knew there would be no way I would be able to concentrate with the racket these ladies were making. They had taken out the Mah-jongg set and were two-bam and three-cracking me to death. And, since I had to get started arranging the cigarette haul sooner or later, I figured this was now sooner. I got on the phone and located Joe Cheese who was my usual banker on these journeys. He had a singles restaurant on the Upper East Side, a western-style place that was usually packed with tight-breasted chicks and horny guys. And, on occasion, Joey. Cheese told me to come over and grab a snack and a snatch.

I sang one quick chorus of "Good Night Ladies," and was out the door.

NEAR MISS?

I took the long route down to Joe Cheese's place. I stayed off the main highways and continually checked my rear-view mirror to see if I had company. I knew I would have to find out who had been tailing me before I hit Squillante, because people who tail people have an awful habit of turning up in the wrong place at the wrong time.

The Cheese's place was not very crowded when I walked in. "Where are all the broads?" I asked.

He shrugged his shoulders. "It's Monday night and it's early. People are recovering from the weekend. We'll do some business later on."

"Fine, then you and I can do some business now. I got orders for cigarettes." The Cheese was one of the biggest shylocks in New York City at this time. We had worked together on a number of things throughout the years, but lately all of our business was in the cigarette field. It was a straight cash deal. He would loan me $80,000 and expect that back plus $15,000 from the profits. If we were arrested, which was very unlikely, it was a straight wash, I didn't owe him any money. My profits, for sending trucks to Carolina, bringing back about 40,000 cartons of cigarettes and distributing them, came to about $10,000. The Cheese made a bigger slice than I did because he was gambling with his money; all I was putting up was my freedom.

It is a profitable way of making a living. The obvious question is, if I'm making $10,000 on cigarettes and not really taking any chances, and $20,000 on a killing in which I'm risking my life, why bother with the killing? There are a few reasons.

First. the only reason I'm in a position to put together a deal like this is because I have a heavyweight reputation. That comes from pulling the trigger, everything else is secondary. When I stop pulling the trigger that rep is gone and with it go many earning opportunities.

Second. there is excitement involved in the doing. I pull the trigger for the same reason people who have become millionaires in the rackets continue to risk going to jail by running two bit bookie or numbers operations. It gets in your blood and becomes the most natural thing to do. I can't imagine anything more boring than running a cigarette smuggling operation every week.

And third and finally, there is more security in pulling the trigger than hauling butts. There have been times when the state troopers and tax people made it too dangerous to bring cigarettes in and I had to stop. There has never been a bad time for killing.

I told Cheese I would need the money Thursday night, cash in full, and he agreed. He told me to meet him at the restaurant and he would have a shopping bag for me. That was his joke.

I told him if the horses I was betting didn't pick up by then he could consider it a going-away present. That was my joke.

It was past 11:30 by this point and I figured the ladies would be getting tired of one another and I could return to my humble abode and get some work done. My timing was not quite right and I had to sit in the bedroom for a few more hands and the last round of coffee and cake. I tried to make the best use of the time by contacting a guy named Bobby Roach who I often did cigarette deals with. Bobby is an arranger, a hustler. He makes things happen. He gets goods and he moves goods, but he is more than a fence because he actively goes out and gets his items. Like cigarettes. And burglar alarms.

"Burglar alarms!" I screamed into the phone, laughing. "You have got to be shitting me."

"No, honest," he said. "There was this truck full of small home burglar alarms that anyone can install, and somehow the truck ended up in one place and the load ended up in another."

Now I had heard absolutely everything. This crook was selling hot burglar alarms.

"Can you maybe get rid of a few for me?" he asked. "We got about six hundred pieces. I priced them and they sell for fifteen bucks and up. We want seven each."

I told him I didn't want anything to do with his hot burglar alarms. Then I told him I had orders for 40,000 cartons of cigarettes and cash to pay for them.

"Whattya want me to do?" he asked.

"Everything. I got some business going and I don't have the time to do this thing right. I'll give you the money and the orders. You get the trucks, pick up the load, bring them back and deliver them. I'll give you five thousand bucks."

"Sounds familiar," he said. And that was it. The Roach could handle this operation because the thing was so smooth it practically ran itself. It didn't require much brainpower, just time. And that is exactly what the Roach had: a little brainpower and a lot of time.

He agreed to start working on the operation and I made arrangements to meet him Thursday night with the money. I wanted the trucks to leave Thursday night so they could be back over the weekend, in time for Monday deliveries.

The house was finally clear when I finished with the Roach. "How'd you do?" I asked my wife and she frowned.

"I lost," she said. The final tab was two dollars and change and she was the big loser. She was very grumpy about it.

"You big-time gamblers are gonna break us," I laughed. At the time I didn't know how lucky she was going to be. A year later she discovered the trotters and one night hit the superfecta for more than $5000. My old lady. It turned out later that there was some talk about the race being fixed, but she didn't know it when she won. And the money still cashed.

But now she'd had a tough night at the table and was going to sleep. This was fine with me, I wanted to sit down and get a good, long look at my notes.

I now have Squillante's routine down as good as I'm going to get it. He follows a very strict schedule every morning and then is somewhat irregular in the afternoon and totally unscheduled at night. That meant, unless I could draw him to me, I was going to have to hit him during his rounds in the morning, near his girlfriend's project or the social club in the afternoon. There were a number of possibilities. I took a clean sheet of white paper and made a list of the places which had potential. In the column next to each place

I listed all the possible problems. In this way I began eliminating different areas.

My major concerns were my ability to get him alone and in the open, the traffic flow in the area and the availability of public transportation. Because this entire job was going to take place in the Bronx where I had grown up and prospered, I knew the traffic patterns reasonably well. While chasing Squillante I had been taking careful notes about stop signs, lights, one-way streets and schools in the area. (You try to mix with a crossing guard lady when school lets out and you will have more trouble than if you get caught pumping bullets into your target.)

Finding a place that insures quick, easy and dependable movement is of the utmost importance. I know of more than one individual who blew a job because they didn't think it through from beginning to end. One particular guy worried about the end, the getaway, more than anything else and worked out a very careful plan. His only problem was he forgot to worry about the beginning. He timed the job so he would be able to make the hit and then meet some people for dinner. His mistake was getting on the East River Drive. There was an accident and he was delayed 35 minutes and missed his target. So he had to have his dinner without the appetizer.

He could have avoided this by staying off main thoroughfares until late at night. Whenever possible I use side streets because I know I can always get through. But there are some things that you simply can't plan for. I blasted a guy in Brooklyn one time, dropped the car I was driving, walked two blocks to the New Lots Avenue subway and got on a train to the Bronx. That should have been it.

But the train got stuck in the tunnel. This was in

the middle of summer and I'm wearing a sports jacket because I've got a cannon tucked into my shirt. So I'm sitting on that train with a just-fired piece which I'm looking to dump, and it's digging into my body. I'm sweating like a stuck pig but there is absolutely no way I can take the jacket off. There is nothing for me to do but sit there and wonder why the train was stuck. Naturally the first thing that popped into my creative mind was that someone had seen me pull the trigger and tailed me to the station and then called the coppers. And they stopped the entire New York City transit system just to get me. It was possible. Eventually the train started moving and there proved to be nothing to worry about. They had stopped for a body on the tracks or something. But my point is that there was absolutely no way I could have planned for that natural mishap.

In looking over my list of potential places to do my work, my first choice had been Hunts Point, but the more I thought about it the less I liked it. The place itself was good, the timing was bad. When he was in the area there was a lot of truck traffic and it was too congested for me to get out as quickly as I thought necessary. Still, a possibility.

His girlfriend's house also had potential but tough problems. She lived on a one-way street which led almost directly to a stop sign and then onto a main thoroughfare. This means I might have to sit there waiting for traffic to let up. Also the Throgs Neck Expressway went right by there, which created much more traffic than I care for. The final thing, which just about eliminated the project from consideration, was the overabundance of kids living in the area. You can never tell when one of them is going to pop up out of nowhere and see something bad for his or her eyes.

The candy store is also a bad traffic area. You have to go down 174th Street which is particularly busy at that hour, and there are a number of one-way streets which cuts down on my choices if I should have to get away quickly. One problem I don't need is the possibility of a head-on collision while I'm trying to leave.

I could have hit him easily when he came out of his apartment building, but I have strong feelings about violating a man's home. I guess it goes back to my own personal experience. I believe a man's home is his sanctuary and that includes areas around it. To me, there is not much difference between hitting a man in his living room, which is forbidden by organization custom, or on his front lawn, which is not.

That left the social club which seemed to have interesting possibilities. There was a good traffic flow. After dark there were not too many people on the streets. Those street lights that still worked were dim. The timing was good in that, according to Sweetlips, he usually left the place after dark. And there were dark doorways I could wait in.

But the negatives outweighed the positives. Number one, I couldn't be sure exactly when he was going to be at the club or when he would leave. He didn't seem to go there at any specific time or stay for any predetermined length. Number two, I saw him leave with another person. This may have been a fluke or Squillante may be a nice guy who drives people home. If it can be avoided you never make a hit when there is only one person with your target. That one person is going to be looking right at you. A restaurant or crowded area is different. There people will usually panic and give 15 different descriptions of you.

Number three, the thing that really eliminated the club was that I remembered it was owned by Jimmy

"Blue Eyes" Alio. I don't think he would be too thrilled if somebody got gunned coming out of his place. Bad for business, naturally. Even though he himself was in the can at this particular time, these were his people running the place and out of respect for him I crossed the social club off my list.

This did not leave me with much. In reality, each of these places had something to offer, as well as drawbacks. I'm positive I could have done the job in any of these places and gotten away with it, but none of them gave me the one thing I was looking for: the dependable edge. The advantage that made the job an unstoppable certainty. With his mundane existence, Joe Squillante was making my work difficult.

Squillante didn't go anywhere alone on a regular basis at night. I would have loved that. Not that I can't work in the daylight. I can and I have. I can work anywhere and anytime. But dark is better for all the obvious reasons. I had absolutely no way of predicting what he did at night. Unless I drew him out and had him come to me.

The more I thought about it the more appealing that idea became. Normally I don't like to do this for two reasons. Whenever you set a guy up you force him to alter his schedule and this in itself may make him wary. Particularly an individual like Squillante, who had a lot to be wary about. And when a man is wary he is on edge and hence much more difficult to surprise.

Second, and worse, setting a person up usually means involving at least one other man and I did not like that at all. Particularly in this case. I don't like other people knowing what I'm doing and, more importantly, when I'm doing it. Specially when those "other people" are Jackie Sweetlips.

Besides the possibility of the double-cross, other people are simply not reliable. I once had a man delivered to me in a vacant field and the jerk who dropped him off just let him out of the car, then drove away. The target took one look around, realized what was happening, and took off like a scared murder victim. I had to run the Kentucky Derby to catch him. When you work by yourself these are problems you just don't have.

So I sat there for an hour weighing the advantages of different areas and different times. I would not really know if I had made the right decision until long after the job had been forgotten. That was always the key. If the job was forgotten I did it right. The wrong decision could cost me a long stay in the Graybar and a reputation amongst my employers that I was getting sloppy. Tentatively I decided to bring him to me. I wasn't sure where, but the Bronx is chock-full of wonderful isolated little pockets that have been used as meeting grounds and body dumpings for more years than I've been around. The thing I had to be careful about was setting myself up for Jackie Sweetlips while I was busy setting up Squillante for the job. I decided to meet with Jackie on Tuesday and see if his fish would swallow my bait.

I called him about fifth thing in the afternoon: Tuesday was a busy day. First and most important on this day, I planned to service my bettors. When they lose I expect them to pay on time and when they win they have every right to expect likewise. Therefore, except on rare occasions, I do not miss.

Tuesday was almost a rare occasion. Very rare.

Before leaving my apartment Tuesday morning I debated changing cars to give me an edge over whoever was trailing me. It would take them some time to pick me up. But I realized I already had an edge: I knew they were there. So I decided to stick with my aging, but comfortable, automobile.

I walked out of my apartment and started toward my car. As I walked I was checking the cars parked up and down the road, seeing if the Chevy was waiting for me. It wasn't in sight.

As I stepped out between two parked cars to cross the street, a yellow cab turned the corner and started down the block. I noticed that the driver had his light on, meaning he had no passengers, and that he was staring right at me. I waited.

He came closer and I took a step back, this guy seemed to be hogging the side of the road I was standing on. He kept coming closer.

He was looking right at me when I knew he was trying to run me down. He couldn't have been more than 75 feet away and I would guess he was traveling about 40 miles per hour. My memory is that he accelerated that last 75 feet.

My reactions were good. I threw my entire body on the hood of the car just behind me, brushing my leg as I landed. I used the momentum of my leap to continue rolling across the hood, until I dropped off the car onto the pavement on the other side. I hit the ground and grabbed the loaded .38 I was carrying.

The cab screeched to a halt, leaving a trail of rubber in the street maybe 30 feet long. The driver came jumping out of the cab and ran towards me. I put my finger on the trigger and aimed.

"Hey, Mac, are you okay?" the driver screamed. Then he saw the gun resting on the hood of the car. He stopped dead in his tracks.

"Don't make a move or I'll blow you away," I said

as calmly as I could. He stuck his hands straight up in the air, like somebody had just rammed a broomstick up his ass.

"Hey, man, I'm really sorry. I've been . . ."

"Shut up!" I ordered. "Lean forward on the car, stretch both your hands out onto the hood." He did just what I told him and then I walked around and gave him a quick shakedown. Nothing on him. I walked to his cab, still keeping an eye on him, and made a perfunctory and fruitless search.

"What the hell was that all about?" I demanded. "You're very lucky to be alive right now." He was in his late forties, I would guess, with graying sideburns and a weathered face. He still had his beret on.

He started to turn around as he began talking. "What happened was . . ."

"Don't move," I said. "I can hear you."

". . . was I've been driving since seven o'clock last night and I guess I just went into a trance. I'm lucky I didn't kill *you*," he said.

I wasn't sure I believed him. "What are you doing in the Bronx?"

"I had a passenger. I just dropped him off."

"Where?" He named a nearby street. It was a legitimate place. His story did seem believable, but he had come too close to killing me. It just would have been too convenient for Sweetlips.

I walked over to his cab door again, reached in and pulled out the hack license. The face in the photograph was lean, had a big mustache and a full head of hair. I looked at the driver. I looked back at the photograph. The driver had no mustache, but he could have shaved it. It could have been his picture. I reached over and pulled off his beret.

He was as bald as a cue ball.

I put the gun into his left ear. "Who the fuck are you?"

"I told you," he said, "I was just . . ."

I pressed the barrel into his ear, twisting it just a touch. Quietly I asked, "If you're the driver then who the fuck is this?" I shoved the license in his face.

He was really scared. "That's my brother-in-law. This is his cab. I take it out some nights. That's all, honest, that's all, I swear."

I just didn't know whether to believe him or not. I stood there, doing nothing.

He kept talking. "Listen, buddy, if I tried to run you down, why would I stop? I woulda kept going if I was trying."

"Maybe you wanted to shoot me."

"Are you crazy? Shoot? Me? Man, I never fired a gun in my life. I don't own a gun! Look, call my brother-in-law and he'll tell you just what I told you."

I released the trigger. He might be telling the truth. There was just no way I could prove it one way or the other. So I had to mark it down as a dangerous accident.

It shook me up a little. I was spending so much time thinking about what Squillante was doing and what Sweetlips might be doing that I was losing touch with what was actually going on. This served as a dangerous reminder.

"Go on," I said testily, "get the fuck out of here. If there's a next time, you're dead." I put the gun away. The cabbie ran to his cab and zoomed down the block. I looked both ways before crossing to my car.

This incident slowed me down a bit. If it was set up by Sweetlips, it was done damn cleverly, and I missed a few of my early customers thinking about it. I did my best to work my way down my sheet. I busted my hump paying and collecting.

And I saved my one problem, Sorry Solly from the garment district, for last. Solly had not been around at the beginning of the previous week for some reason, but he got on the phone when I called Thursday and guaranteed he would have the $3000 he owed me by Tuesday. Now it's Tuesday and I'm calling and I'm being told he isn't in. I knew I was getting the runaround, so I went visiting.

His place was on the third floor of an old building on 29th Street just off Seventh Avenue. He was standing right in the showroom, displaying some merchandise for a customer, when I walked in. When he saw me he was obviously unhappy but there was no great display of emotions. He just excused himself from his customer and took me into his office.

Physically, Solly was just what you would expect in the garment district. He was about five-feet six-inches tall, thin and had a full head of white hair. I would guess he was in his early sixties, but there was really no way of telling.

"Look," I said, "I don't like to come up to a guy's place unless . . ."

He interrupted me. "It's okay. Listen, I got a problem. I don't have your money." It was obvious he didn't want to waste any time either. "See, I had to borrow money for my spring line which is doing well, but people just aren't paying their bills on time."

"You could've told me that three weeks ago. What the hell you been putting me off for?" Now I'm getting mad but I'm still trying not to lose my temper.

He shrugged his shoulders. "I kept expecting the

money to come in. And it's coming, but I've got to pay my suppliers too, you know."

"I know, I know," I said. "But if you knew you couldn't pay what the fuck did you keep betting for? You're costing me time and money. What do I need you for?"

"If I knew why I kept betting I'd stop betting and then I wouldn't owe you the money, right?" He paused. "Listen, you got to give me one more week. Next week . . ."

That was exactly what I didn't want to hear. I guess the strain of my near accident finally came out. "I don't want to hear any more of that next week crap. I want my money and I want it now."

"I don't have it. What are you going to do, kill me for three thousand bucks?" All of a sudden he's a wiseguy.

"Okay smartass. I ain't gonna kill you. I'm gonna do you a favor. I'll be back Thursday afternoon and I'm gonna take you to meet a man who is going to lend you the money you owe me. And then . . ."

He cut in. "You mean a shylock? I will not . . ."

"Don't interrupt me when I'm telling you something. I ain't askin', I'm tellin'. I'm gonna take you to meet this guy and you and I are gonna settle up for good. I don't want you betting with me no more." I started to get up. "Let me tell you something else. If you had been a gentleman about this thing, if you had answered my phone calls today or told me the story three weeks ago, I woulda worked something out with you. Now you can go fuck yourself. You be here Thursday afternoon."

Solly sat there sort of stunned. I don't think he was used to having people give him orders. And we both knew I wasn't kidding. I walked out and left him sitting here.

I drove over to Jackie's lot and he wasn't there. So I left word that a friend of Petey's had been by to see him and wanted to talk about a possible deal, and that I would meet him at the Half Moon around 11 P.M.

Thus far it had been a very frustrating day and I really needed something to get my rocks off. I needed to fire a gun. So this was a perfect time to test fire the weapon that I planned to kill Squillante with. The test firing would take place in a safe basement in Yonkers. But before I went I decided to take a quick swing by Squillante's place and see if my boy was home safely.

On the way I continually checked my rear-view mirror, but there didn't seem to be anyone on my tail.

When I reached Squillante's apartment I double-parked under a tree, hiding myself within its shadow so Mrs. Gibson couldn't see me, and watched. I sat there maybe five minutes and then the door opened and someone walked out. In the shadow of the building it was difficult to see who it was, but for some reason the walk looked familiar. I watched as he got closer, feeling safe because my car was completely hidden. He came closer and closer, although he didn't look in my direction. He didn't have to.

He was about 30 yards away when I recognized him.

Jackie Sweetlips was leaving Squillante's apartment!

THE BEST LAID PLANS

There is a well-known basement in the city of Yonkers which is virtually soundproof. This basement belongs to an individual named Charlie who had the foresight to soundproof the walls when he purchased a brand new split-level home in the early 1960s. Charlie is an amiable sort of fellow who will let people use his basement for a small fee. For an additional small fee he will even cater your affair. From time to time people who have run into problems with other people have been taken down to Charlie's basement for a discussion. I use the place for percussion.

I wanted to test the gun I had gotten from Cockeyed Jimmy to find out what I could expect from it. I wanted to know how dependable it was. Normally I go up to Charlie's maybe four times a year, even when I have nothing on tap, to fire a few rounds from different weapons just to keep them in working shape. So Charlie did not think there was anything unusual happening when I called and asked him if his basement was busy. He said it wasn't and invited me to visit.

I stopped back at my place and picked up the new gun and three different types of ammunition. At this point in history I kept a lot of ammunition in my dresser drawer because I had some trouble finding a steady supplier in New York City. Since gunshops in New York were required to take your name and address when they sold you ammunition, I used to have to go way upstate to a little place outside Monticello to stock up. (This is the supplier who makes the special cartridges for my hand shotgun.) Since I had only used a few rounds in the last couple of months I had plenty of ammo on hand.

Normally I would put the gun in a brown paper bag and the bullets in my pocket, because I don't like to leave the house with a loaded weapon. But with all the strange happenings I didn't want to take any chances. Although I was already carrying a loaded .38, I loaded the new gun too, and stuck it in my pocket. I keep a loaded gun by my dresser and another one hidden by the front door at all times. If I have any unusual company all I have to do is reach for one of them. And if I should walk out of my front door with a loaded gun and a cop grabs me it's a felony. If the gun isn't loaded it's a misdemeanor. I am a very cautious individual. I know the law. I try to play each angle. That may sound overly dramatic, but it is my life I'm playing with.

On the way to Charlie's basement I stopped at a lumberyard where I picked up four pieces of wood: one 2 x 4, one 3 x 6, one 1" board and a solid piece of plywood. These would serve as my laboratory equipment.

Charlie was waiting for me when I got there and before going downstairs to business we sat and shot the shit for awhile. Then I went down to the basement to work. I set up each board against a cement wall and stepped back about eight feet. Eight feet was the furthest possible distance I would be from Squillante when I hit him. I like to be right up close, range zero, because then there is no possibility of missing, but plenty close enough to guarantee results.

I had three different types of cartridges with me because I wanted to test them all. The first was a hollow-point bullet which will cut you to ribbons once it penetrates the skin; the second type was the flat-nosed or flat-head type and the third was your regular ball bullet. I started by emptying out the shells I had put in the new .38, and replacing them with four hollow-point bullets. Then I fired one bullet into each board. I repeated this with the other two types of ammunition.

Then I moved closer until I was about three feet away and did exactly the same thing. When I finished doing that my testing was completed, now I had to interpret the results.

First, I know the gun is good as soon as the first shot is fired. Second, when I dig the remains of the bullets out of the wood I can pretty well predict what is going to happen to the bullet in Squillante's body. I wanted to make sure that there would be no fragments which could be traced back to this gun. If the police can't match gun and bullets, it makes it much more difficult for them to put a case together.

As a rule, ball ammunition will come out whole, flat ammunition will come out pretty well flattened and wide, like a piece of squashed dough, and the hollow-point ammunition will splatter because it spreads as it goes into the wood. The piece of wood I'm really interested in is the plywood because that has a resistance that most resembles the human head. The plywood had been shattered into pieces.

The results of my tests were conclusive: The gun is

excellent and I had my choice of ammunition. Although I knew there was a chance I would change my mind, I decided to use the hollow-point bullet.

I went back upstairs and sat with Charlie while I cleaned the gun. Weapons are his hobby and we talked guns and then gun-control legislation. Charlie told me that the general opinion of the pro-gun people was that nothing was going to happen about gun control and that I shouldn't worry about it. I promised him I wouldn't.

The use of Charlie's basement was $25. The advice was free. Both were worth exactly what I paid for them.

That left only one more thing I had to get done this day, meet with Jackie Sweetlips. I had three things on my mind that Jackie could settle: One, would Squillante go along if Jackie told him to go to a meet? Two, who was tailing me? And three, what the fuck had he been doing at Squillante's place?

I wasn't about to ask him questions two and three straight out. If he was planning to burn me, I didn't want to let him know I was on to him. If he was indeed planning such a mistake, the one advantage I had was that I knew he was, and I knew he would tie it in with my hitting Squillante. As long as I knew that, I could exercise some control. But if Jackie found out I was on to him he would move quickly and when I wasn't waiting for him, so I couldn't let on I was suspecting things.

A plan began to develop in my mind. The more specific I was with Jackie about where I would be with Squillante, the more control I would have. I could turn things around on him. If he thought I was in one place

I could be in another place, nearby, and watch him make his best move.

I could still kill Squillante. And if Sweetlips moved, him too. This job was beginning to have some real appeal to me.

I drove over to the Half Moon right from Charlie's basement. On occasion I would backtrack a few blocks, just to make sure I wasn't being followed, but I still managed to get there by 10:30. Jackie Sweetlips didn't wander in until 11:15. I was deep into my cherry cheesecake by that time.

He nodded to me and I returned his nod. We sat and small-talked until I finished my dessert and then left together. We got in my car and drove up the West Side Drive to the Saw Mill River Parkway and headed upstate. It is nice and quiet in an automobile and if you're careful where you drive, you don't have to worry about being seen by anybody.

"What's your problem?" he asked after we settled down for the drive. His tongue stayed firmly inside his mouth.

I hesitated because I wanted to make sure I used exactly the right words. I didn't want to start him worrying about anything. "It's not exactly a problem," I said carefully, "more of a complication. This job is going to be a little trickier than I thought. So far Squillante's routine is difficult. I got half a dozen places I can take him, but I really don't like any of them. And he really doesn't do anything at night, at least nothing I can depend on."

Sweetlips stared straight ahead. "So what do you want me to do?"

"I'll get to that," I told him. "Don't be so damn impatient."

He turned toward me. "Don't you tell me what to do."

I could see he was getting uptight. I decided to back down, something I'm not used to doing, because I didn't want a confrontation in the front seat of my car. "Okay, okay," I said, "I'm sorry." I drove on in silence for a few more minutes. "Does Squillante have any idea at all what is going on?"

"No fucking way." That sounded positive enough.

"How about those two yo-yos. Is it possible they tipped him?"

Jackie chuckled. "They seem to be happy living and I don't think they want to jeopardize that. In fact," he continued, "they met with him yesterday to talk about the next job."

A bell of recognition started ringing in my head. I asked him, "You wouldn't happen to know where they met with him, would you?"

"Yeah, I know. Squillante has a piece of a beauty parlor in Manhattan. They met in a back room there."

"Isn't that something!" I said to myself as much as to Sweetlips. "I saw him go into the place and then I saw these guys a little while later. I couldn't figure out what the hell he was up to."

"Now you know."

"Now I know," I agreed.

He sighed. Then he started speaking. "There are a few problems though. If you hadn't called me I was going to contact you."

"I'm listening."

He paused for a minute before he spoke, so when he did it sounded very dramatic. "Squillante is getting ready to make a move."

"What kind of move?"

"We don't know. But he told the boys this was going to be the last job . . ."

"Maybe he's just scared," I interrupted.

He glared at me. "Will you let me fuckin' finish?"

"I'm sorry, I'm sorry. Okay."

"Jesus," he said, shaking his head. If he was acting, he was overacting. If he wasn't acting, he was really as much of a jerk as I thought he was. "He cashed in all his bank accounts Friday. He's got a lot of cash on hand."

"I was with him Friday," I said. "I didn't see him go near any banks."

Sweetlips was quick on the uptake. "I mean, it was his wife, closed them all down. He's got more than sixty-five thousand in cash on hand."

"Well, whattya think?"

"I think he's gonna start running." *Now* his tongue came shooting out of his mouth.

"When do you think?"

"We're not sure. He told the boys he wants them to work next Monday. So it won't be until next week at the earliest."

"So how come he took the money out so early?" I was trying to be cute as well as careful. I never took my eyes off the road.

Jackie shook his head from side to side. "Maybe he's the nervous type. Anyway, the Fat Man wants to know what you're going to do about it."

It was interesting that he said the "Fat Man" wanted to know, not that Jackie Sweetlips did. "I guess I'll have to move before then." They were putting me in a time box.

"When?"

It didn't really bother me because I had decided that, for my own safety, I wanted them to know precisely when and where I was going to make my move. That way, if they were going to make a move, I could figure when they were going to make it. How else could they be guaranteed of getting me in a lonely place by myself? "Right now I'm thinking about the weekend. Okay, Jackie, listen up now. If you tell Squillante to do something, will he do it?"

Sweetlips nodded. "He's good at following orders. If we tell him to lay on his stomach and quack like a duck, the only question he'll ask is 'how loud?' "

I checked the rear-view mirror, even going through Brewster, N.Y., but I was as clean as a whistle. "That's good," I agreed. "Now, if I tell you that, on a certain night, say Saturday night for argument's sake, I want him to meet somebody somewhere, you think you could make sure he would be there?"

Jackie answered very slowly and distinctly. "Quack, quack," he said.

"Are you sure?" He nodded. "Okay, I'll tell you where and when after I figure it out." We drove on in silence as I formulated the plan for Squillante. Before I opened my mouth again I turned the car around and headed back down the parkway. "Okay, I want you to tell Squillante that there's a job to do and he's been chosen to do the job. Tell him it's no rough-house, it's just that he has to be able to identify some-body." I explained the plan in detail. Squillante was going to be told to meet a man at a certain location, and then they would go to a second location where he was to point somebody out to this guy. Jackie said he would offer a couple of extra geezles for the job, just to make sure Squillante didn't get suspicious. We both knew he would have to be suspicious as hell, but would have to go or take the bigger risk of a long talk with the Fat Man.

As we drove back I really wanted to ask Jackie about the tail and his visit to Squillante's house. But he didn't bring it up or give me any sort of opening. I tried to create one. "What's he been acting like at the office?"

"Like Squillante. Friendly." He thought for a minute. "Maybe he's been a little quieter than normal."

"And outside the office?"

He looked right at me. His tongue came shooting out of his mouth. "How the hell should I know?"

I shrugged my shoulders. "I don't know. I just thought maybe you did." I was sort of surprised he hadn't given up the tail and told me about it. Since they had not followed me again I thought they must have realized I picked them up. That meant that if Sweetlips was behind it, he knew that I had picked it up. But he said nothing.

As he was getting out of the car in the parking lot at the Half Moon he said he personally liked the plan, but he would have to get the final okay from the Fat Man. He didn't expect any problem. I expressed my appreciation for his optimism.

Tuesday had been a long day and more questions had been asked rather than answered. There was no question that Sweetlips's information would force me to move very quickly on Squillante. The only question was whether Sweetlips gave me that information to make me move toward my own grave, or if he gave it to me because it was true. Something else I didn't have the answer to.

In any case, the end was now in sight. I had tested the gun and selected a plan that would work under normal circumstances. Now all I had to do was find the proper place, and that would be Wednesday's chore.

Instead of going straight home I decided to detour to Pelham Bay and make sure Mr. Squillante was tucked away for the evening. Now that the hit was actually getting underway I didn't want anything except me to happen to him. It is terribly frustrating to get yourself all psyched up for a job and have it fall through for some reason or another. This had happened to me before. I once spent two weeks tailing a guy and decided to hit him on the way to his girlfriend's apartment. He made a practice of stopping there every single night, which is somewhat unusual, but this is what he did. The big day came and I'm sitting and waiting and waiting and he never shows up.

I raced over to his house and his car is gone and the place is pitch black. It was obvious my man had been tipped off and had flown, so I called the man who hired me to give him the bad news. It turned out to be good news. The man who hired me told me my target had suffered a heart attack that morning and wasn't expected to live. He did live though, long enough for me to catch up to him and stop his heart permanently.

I did not expect to have that sort of problem with Squillante. When I drove by his place the lights were on in the living room and his car was parked for the night, doors locked. Feeling contented, I went home myself.

I spent some time Tuesday night lying awake in bed wondering where to have Squillante meet me. Having a free choice of spots makes you work hard—there are just so many possible places. Just when you think you've found the perfect place another area pops into your head and the whole process begins again.

The most important thing to look for is isolation.

If you can have it, why shouldn't you? Why hit a guy on a street in the Bronx when you can hit him on a beach or under a bridge, in a cemetery or even a junkyard? The only other thing you have to consider is the spot must be believable to the intended. If Sweetlips told Squillante he was supposed to meet somebody on a sand dune in Long Beach, Squillante would think twice because a beach is just too perfect a setup. So what I am actually looking for is a not-so-seemingly-perfect perfect spot.

It kept me tossing and turning for a few hours. Every time I closed my eyes I would think of another possible spot and start running down its potential. I was working harder just lying there than I did when I was in my car.

I guess this disturbed my wife. "Whatever it is," she finally said, "can't it wait till tomorrow?" Then she went to sleep. She has a way of getting off these one-liners then konking out immediately.

Not me.

Wednesday started out to be a nice, lazy day. First thing I did was call my bookmaking office and set up a meeting to settle for the week. I had the money and there was no reason not to get it out of the way. But before I left the house I asked my wife about Sunday night. "Are the Squillantes still coming for dinner?"

"I assume so," she said. "I haven't spoken to Cindy since I told you."

I asked her, "Do me a favor? Call her sometime today and let me know if they're still coming."

She wanted to know why.

"Because," I told her.

"What kind of an answer is that?" she said.

I lost my temper. "Just do it! I don't need a reason for everything, do I? Just call her and find out, huh?"

She agreed. I don't know what I expected to find out from this, but there was always the chance of gaining some information. If Mrs. Squillante said they couldn't come I would at least have reason to believe Sweetlips was telling the truth, they were packing to leave. On the other hand, if she said they were, that wouldn't tell me anything. It's possible they aren't leaving until later in the week, it's possible she doesn't even know he's leaving, it's possible she's going to call later in the week and cancel, it's possible they just aren't planning to show up.

Anything is possible.

After driving down to the bookmaking outfit and settling up I picked up on Squillante just as he was leaving the coffee shop. I was with him perhaps a half-hour when I looked in my rear-view mirror. The Chevy was back.

I dropped off Squillante quickly. The Chevy did not follow. I parked for a minute and tried to analyze the facts. The Chevy picked me up twice, both times when I was tailing Squillante. Therefore it seems obvious the Chevy is with Squillante. Or against him. But in any case it is following him, at least until I get on the scene. If they were friends of his watching his tail, my cover should have been blown. He should be running, or at least screaming. And he wasn't doing anything of the sort. The only conclusion I could draw was that the tail was not with Squillante, but rather following him. So it could only come from Sweetlips. The question is why? Sweetlips still doesn't like me from long ago? The Fat Man doesn't trust me?

I stopped in at Johnny Dee's for some weak coffee, a stale donut, and some bad jokes. Even though this job was getting very complicated, and I was spending an awful lot of time on it just driving and thinking, I still couldn't forsake my other businesses. Or my love life. I called the Roach to find out what our cigarette customers were doing. They were doing good, he told me. "Don't forget I want you to save a few hundred cartons for my wife and her friends," I reminded him.

"Tell me how many you want so I can write an order."

I thought for a minute. "Leave me seven-fifty. If that turns out to be too much I'll hustle them to a machine vendor."

"Seven-fifty," the Roach said. "Your wife is gonna have a hell of a smoker's cough." Everybody's a comedian.

We made arrangements to meet at the warehouse Thursday night so I could give him the cash and send the drivers on their merry way. Next I gambled that my sweet Alice had been too lazy to work this afternoon and tried her apartment. One for me. "I had a real bad headache this morning," she said, "and I'm only just getting out of bed."

"Don't bother," I said. By the time I got there she had put it together enough to have a bathrobe on, the slinky fake-satin kind that you can imagine right through.

"How do you feel?" I thought I was being solicitous of her condition.

She put her hand on my balls and squeezed gently. "Like that," she said. "How else?"

Some days everybody is a comedian. I mean *everybody*.

I had a full night's work ahead of me so I only stopped home briefly. My old lady didn't have anything on the stove. She had been over at my brother's house all afternoon with my sister-in-law. My nephew, it turned out, had gotten into glue sniffing and they were trying to decide what to do about it. I told my wife she should butt out, this was their concern, and we discussed it loudly for a few minutes. "If your brother asked you what to do about it, what would you tell him?" she yelled, emphasizing the "you."

"I'd tell him to bat the kid's head against the wall a few times," I yelled right back, "and knock a little brains into his head! That's what I would do," emphasizing the "I."

She calmed down enough to ask me if I wanted some dinner.

I just wanted to get out of that place. I told her, "No, I been eating all day." It was no lie. "Hey, did you speak to Cindy Squillante?"

She nodded. "They're coming. I told them to get here about seven-thirty. Is that okay with you?"

It was okay with me, I told her. And then I left.

My task for the evening was going to be to find *the* place for the big finale. I waited until night because I knew the job was going to be done at night. Places that look great in the daylight have a way of becoming very bad in the dark. Maybe a streetlight reflects over the area, maybe traffic is rerouted through there for some reason, maybe honest citizens use the spot to walk their dogs. But if you're going to move at night, you have to see the spot at night.

I had two particular places in mind, both of them in the Bronx, both of them known safe meeting places. The first spot was in Hunts Point, right near a cardboard-box factory. I drove over there and parked across the street. And I sat and I waited. It didn't take me long to discover problems. One, there was an all-night grocery store nearby and a steady stream of cabbies came down the block. (I assumed the owner was also taking numbers on the side.) Secondly, there were at least two night watchmen within sight of the spot, one in the box factory, the other in a warehouse. And third, Hunts Point was considered by the police a "high crime area," and thus was heavily patrolled. That meant a cop car could come steaming down the block at any time.

On the positive side there were plenty of places for me to hide, a free traffic flow, enough crime in the area that the local citizenry was not about to come running when they thought they saw something happening, and finally Squillante would not be suspicious when told to meet someone there.

I moved to my next choice, a dead end near Bronx Park and 182nd Street, where the Boston Road temporarily ends and the park begins. There is a heavily shaded area, which is particularly dark at night, almost cut right out of the park, and this has long been a favorite meeting and greeting spot. I knew the area well because at one time I ran numbers here.

There was a lot to recommend it: One, a free flow of traffic; two, this is a tough area and no one is about to come running even if they think something nasty-nasty is happening; three, it was pretty deserted at night; four, the cops had always tended to stay away; five, I knew the area, all the side streets and all the entrances to highways and expressways; and six, since this place was a known meeting ground, Squillante would not give it too much thought when told to meet someone there.

The only possible negative factor was an apartment building sitting almost directly across the street. Even that wasn't a real problem, though, because only a few rear windows looked down on the spot, and the area was so poorly lit I didn't think anyone could see much anyway.

I parked my car and started walking around the block. It was only nine o'clock and there was almost no movement on the street. It was so quiet you could hear the traffic from upper Boston Road. I walked right into the building and up to the roof. New York City roofs are used for just about everything from sunbathing to balling. This one seemed to be used mostly for storing metal objects that would rust, like old bicycles and tire rims. It was empty and dirty and not the type of place anyone would come for a breath of fresh air. Looking over the side, I stared at the spot and had my judgment confirmed: It was almost completely blacked out from the building.

I went down and sat in my car and waited. I waited for people walking their dogs. I waited for cars to go by and light the area with their headlights. I waited for a patrol car. I waited for some kids to park and make it. Two cars went by. No patrol cars came near the place. No dogs. No kids. I made my decision: This is the spot where Joe Squillante would die.

Now only one blank had to be filled in: When? I started calculating in my head. It had to be before Monday night. Jackie Sweetlips would need a couple of days to arrange the meeting. I would have to get a car. Thursday night was out; it was too close and I had too many things to do already. I'd need Friday night to steal the car. That brought me up to Saturday, with Sunday to fall back on in case something went wrong. Saturday night would be perfect. Now all the pieces were fitting together. On Saturday night I would shoot Joe Squillante with a .38, using hollow-point bullets, just past the intersection of 182nd Street and Boston Road.

As I slowly drove back to my place I went over the plan in my mind. Twice. Three times. It seemed perfect. I was looking for loopholes, but there just didn't seem to be any. Squillante would be told to show up at the spot Saturday night at 11 P.M. He would be told he was to meet a man and take him somewhere, the man would tell him where, and then point out an individual he was familiar with. He would, in fact, be waiting for me.

I would arrive early and, although I would tell Sweetlips I was going to wait in my car, I would be waiting in the building. That way I could see everything happening in front of me. After Squillante arrived I would let him sit for awhile, then I'd just walk up to the car and blow his brains out. Then I would follow my usual pattern of getting rid of the gun.

My wife didn't even mention my crummy glue-sniffing nephew to me when I got home. We talked about a number of things. "What would you like me to serve Sunday night?" she asked.

"Don't worry about it," I told her, "you'll think of something." Actually, if everything went right, she wouldn't have to bother.

I waited until she went to bed and then I took out my notes one more time. I looked them over very carefully and decided there was nothing in them that I needed. So I got myself a metal wastebasket from the kitchen and burned them until they were nothing but ashes.

With the burning of the notes the planning stage ended and the action phase began. On every hit, up until this point, there is always something hazy, something unreal about it. It's like a big jigsaw puzzle, you are so concerned with finishing one small section you never bother to picture what the whole thing will look like. You work on one section, then another, and another, until the whole thing begins to come together. When you plan a job you never think of the end result. It's not so much a murder as it is a game. Planning the perfect hit. You never think that the man you watch, the man you trail, is going to cease to exist at the time and place you choose for his execution.

It is when the planning ends that the so-called deadly game begins. This is when reality strikes home. You realize the enormous power you have. You realize that you are about to become the most important man in the victim's life, although he will have less than a second to know that. You are going to be the last thing he sees before he dies.

It is mostly a wonderful feeling, as well as frightening.

I wondered if Squillante would have time to consider the fates that brought us together. Two guys who grew up in the same neighborhood, who followed generally the same paths, who knew generally the same people. Of all the guys he would guess would be there when he died, I would be his last guess. I was curious to see how he would react when he saw me, if he had time to recognize me.

In a strange way I hoped he did. I very rarely get to play to an audience that knows my name.

NEAR MRS.

With the planning finished there was little for me to
do but set the thing in motion. I did this by driving
over to see Jackie first thing Thursday morning, 11
o'clock. That is the first time when I can work it out.

We walked up Jerome Avenue together, and then
around the corner. This was just in case anyone was
interested in our conversation. "The Fat Man says it's
okay with him," he said. "He left it up to me to get
him there."

"You sure you can?"

"Yeah, I'm sure. You tell me where and he'll be
there. That's all."

"It sounds too easy to me," I said. "I mean, if I was
doing what he was doing, I'd think twice about going
to any kind of meetin'."

Jackie stopped walking and turned to me. "Look.
You told me to get him, I'll get him there, okay? The
guy is in a bind, he can't say no. If I tell him the Fat
Man wants him to do somethin', he's gonna do it. It
really is as simple as that. Now you just worry about
your end and leave mine alone, okay?"

"Okay," I answered, "but just make sure you get
him there. It gets fuckin' cold out at night."

He looked at me in a nasty tone, but didn't say anything. I decided to push ahead. "Okay, here's what I want. The spot is where Boston Road dead ends at Bronx Park. If he don't know how to get there, tell him to take 182nd Street right to the end. There's a little spot that has trees all around it and it's pretty dark.

"Tell him to take his own car and be there by eleven o'clock. Tell him you don't care what time he leaves his place, but he better be there by eleven. When he gets there all he has to do is make sure the door on the passenger side of the car is open and sit there and wait. Tell him that somebody he is familiar with, just tell him it's a friend, don't tell him it's me no how, is going to meet him there. Tell him they will drive to another location and he will point somebody out to his friend. That's all."

I paused. My next sentence was strictly for Jackie. I wanted to make sure he would know exactly where I was going to be, even though, in actuality, I wouldn't be there at all. "I'm going to be sitting about fifteen yards away from the spot in my own car. I'll stay low and he won't see me. I'll pop out and walk over to him and end it." I turned to Jackie. "Will he go for this?"

"He will when I put two thou behind the Fat Man's order."

We walked on for a few more minutes with neither of us saying anything. I knew he didn't like being there with me, but his mind seemed to be on the project. "I'll never understand Squillante," he said all of a sudden. "The guy was making good money, doing good things, and he gets himself messed up." He paused. "You know, the guy is not the worst in the world and he works hard. I'll be sorry to see him go."

I wasn't sure if that speech was for my benefit or not, the final convincing words designed to make me feel Sweetlips was a guy with a big heart, and forget that Sweetlips might rather see me dead than Squillante. I wasn't feeling quite so sympathetic. "We all got to go sometime."

"Listen," he said, "you need a driver or a car for this thing?"

I didn't want any more help from him at all. "Thanks for the offer," I said kindly, "but no thanks."

He shrugged. "Have it your way."

We walked back to the lot and started to separate. Just before we said our good-byes I told him I would call him Saturday morning just to check in with him.

We nodded to each other. "Saturday," he said, "he'll be there."

"Quack, quack?" I asked.

"Quack, quack," he agreed.

Thursday was going to be another busy day. The first part of my other work consisted of taking a ride with Sorry Solly.

I drove down to his place to pick him up. In the back of my mind I really didn't think it would be necessary. Solly is a man who understands what shylocks are and what it means to be in to them, so I figured he would have my $3000 for me.

I was wrong. "What can I tell you?" he tried to con me. "I couldn't get it. But if you just give me a few more days I can . . ."

"I heard that joke already," I interrupted, "get your coat. We're gonna meet a friend of mine."

He sat there behind his desk debating what he

should do. His problem was that he just didn't know how serious I was. All he knew was what he saw on television and in the movies, what he had read in books and magazines, so he didn't know if I was bluffing. "What would you do if I didn't go with you?" It was a simple question, not meant as a challenge or a threat.

I answered just as simply. "I'd hurt ya." I stopped to let that sink in. "And then we'd still take this trip."

He realized it was inevitable and grabbed his coat. We hopped in a cab—his treat—and went to a pizza parlor in Greenwich Village between Bleecker and Sullivan Streets. The individual who runs this place is named Tony and between pizza tosses he loans out money at what the legal profession would call "exorbitant interest rates." In other words, anybody who borrows from him is going to pay well for that privilege.

I don't know Tony that well, although we've done some business. I took Solly there because it was the closest place I knew that would have the money on hand for this type of loan. I ordered two Sicilian slices, one for me and one for Solly—my treat—and told Tony we had some business we would like to discuss with him. He told us to go sit in one of the small booths in the back.

I made the introductions when he sat down. "Tony, this is Solly and he wants to borrow some money from you."

Tony nodded to Solly. "How much you want?"

I said, "Three thousand bucks." Normally when I trade a man off I take less than what is owed to me in exchange for the actual cash money. This is the way I pay the shy for his services. But in this case I was so pissed at Sorry Solly for screwing me around I decided to take my whole cut.

Tony looked at Solly again. "How you want to work this?"

Solly didn't know what he was talking about. "What do you mean?"

"I mean, how do you want to pay me? How long do you want to take? How much can you pay each week?" In the end they agreed on a two year loan, which was really too long. I never bothered to check, but I assume Solly made his payments. In all, they would have come to close to $9000, just to pay off a $3000 debt!

Tony paid me the cash right then and there. Poor Sorry Solly was so unhappy to be part of this transaction that I doubt he ever bet again. I know he didn't bet with me. We took a cab back up to his place—his treat—and he started talking. I didn't care. I had my money, I wasn't mad at him anymore. "What happens if I can't pay him back? If I miss one of the payments?" He said it in a very nervous tone.

"He's an easy guy to get along with. He'll work with ya."

"But, I mean, what if I can't pay him back his money?"

"Then he'll hire someone like me to hurt ya. See pal, you can't win. That's what you get for being a louse. I gave you more than enough time to start getting straightened out with me and you didn't even make an attempt. You give me a song and dance, you don't answer the goddam phone, and then you want to dictate terms to me.

"Let me tell you something, Solly baby. I just did you the biggest favor. I taught you how expensive the game can be. You should thank me for it."

He laughed unhappily. "Thank you," he said politely, but I don't think he really meant it.

Half the money I had belonged to the office, but I didn't see any great hurry to run right over and deliver it. I'd just include it in the following week's payments.

By late afternoon I had some time to kill before meeting the Cheese. I really didn't know what to do. Sometimes it's easier to kill a guy than an hour. I went bowling by myself for awhile. At one point I was a good bowler but I had gotten out of practice. I throw a good hard ball and when I'm not rolling regularly I tend to lose control of it. I bowled four games, none with startling results, and I had enough of that.

One thing about people who work the way I do, hit and miss, on and off, is that they have a lot of free time to fill. It gets very hard to find enough things to do that keep you interested. I think this is one reason a lot of people get into the horses and other sports. Betting can be an occupation by itself. You've got to take time to study the sheets, then you've got the excitement of the event itself and then you check the results. This takes hours and, if you do it right, it never gets boring.

In this particular case I decided to swing by Squillante's place one more time, just to make sure everything was still sweet. I pulled up to my lamppost and started sitting. His car was parked a little ways up the block from mine and there was a light on in his apartment. I waited. Ten minutes.

I watched. The door opened and I was astonished! I could not believe what was walking out of that door. It was Mrs. Gibson with one of the biggest animals I ever seen in my life. She had a long chain around its neck and seemed to be fully in control.

She waved as she got near to the car. "Look what we have for you," she said in her sing-song grandmother voice. "Look what we found for yo-ou."

I didn't get out of the car. I pointed at the Great Dane. "What's that?"

The smile left her face. "This is your dog." She looked right at me. I looked right back at her. She finished the sentence by raising her eyebrows. "Isn't it?"

I shook my head slowly from side to side. "It's too dark. I never saw that dog before in my life." I leaned out the window to look at the dog a little more closely. Without any warning the animal jumped against the car, opened his mouth and started licking my face. He could also have taken off my head. He was that big.

"My, my," she said happily, "look how she loves you. Are you sure this isn't your dog?"

"Look, Mrs. Gibson, honest, this isn't my dog. I mean, I really appreciate this and everything, but this just isn't my dog."

Maybe she thought I was lying. "How do you know?"

"Whattya mean how do I know. I know my own dog, don't I? And this isn't it. It's the wrong color, for starters. Too dark."

She didn't know what to say. "You mean I've been keeping this dog in my apartment for four days and it isn't even yours." She stopped, opened her mouth and asked with great uneasiness, "Then whose is it?"

I gave her a blank look. "Where'd you get it?"

"A teen-ager brought it to me and said he saw my reward sign and . . ."

"Reward sign?"

"Oh, yes, I didn't want to tell you, but I put up a ten-dollar reward to get the dog back."

Inside I was laughing hysterically. I knew exactly what happened. "Mrs. Gibson, I'm not sure how to tell you this. But I think what you got there is a hot dog." I said it very carefully, making sure to separate the words "hot" and "dog."

She didn't pick up. "A hot dog?"

I corrected myself. "A stolen dog. The kid read the poster and took the dog when somebody tied him up outside or something." I could see she was really worried.

"You mean I could be arrested?"

"I'm afraid so, unless you return the dog immediately."

"Where? Where?"

I told her to call the ASPCA or the police and they would probably have a missing dog report. Then I reached into my pocket and took out a ten-dollar bill. "You're a lovely lady Mrs. Gibson," I said, "and I want you to know I appreciate you worrying about my poor little dog and trying to find her for me and my children." I handed her the bill. "Now you go inside and call the police."

"You're right, Mr. Gold, perfectly right. And I want you to know that I'll keep looking for your dog until we find her. Poor thing." She started walking away. "I promise you, Mr. Gold, I promise."

"That's good, Mrs. Gibson, that's nice." Just at that moment the dog must have seen something that interested it because all of a sudden it took off running, with poor, nice Mrs. Gibson doing her very best to keep hold of the leash attached to her stolen dog. As they disappeared around the corner I stopped laughing long enough to pull away and head home for dinner.

On the way home my idiot mistake dawned on me. I was so busy being a smartass I had put the one person who can identify me and place me on Squillante's block in touch with the police.

A very, very silly thing to do.

The little woman was not there, but she had the foresight to let some chop meat thaw out so I could make hamburgers. I was mixing Joey's famous hamburger sauce when the telephone rang. "Hello?"

"Joey?"

"Yeah."

"This is Squillante, Joe Squillante."

I fumbled for a reply. "Yeah? Well, what's happening?"

"Nothing much. What's happening with you?"

"Same thing. Nothing much. I didn't expect to hear your voice when I picked up the phone."

"Oh?"

"I thought maybe it was my old lady. She isn't here and I didn't know where she was." I couldn't figure out what in the world Squillante was calling me about. My mind was racing in two directions as I spoke to him, one trying to make the normal conversation, the other trying to understand the call.

"I'm sorry she's not there. Actually I'm calling to tell you that Cindy and I can't make it Sunday night."

I was thrilled. "Oh, that's too bad," I said as realistically as I could, "my wife was looking forward to seeing your wife. What'sa matter?"

His voice was calm and level. "Nothing really. It's just that my mother was supposed to take care of the children all day but now she's had a very mild heart attack . . ."

"I'm sorry to hear that."

162

He laughed. "It's nothing really. She has one every time she thinks I'm taking my wife somewhere and not her." We both laughed. "Anyway, we're probably going to be spending Sunday visiting her in the hospital so we thought we'd better cancel now."

"Don't worry about it," I said graciously, "I'm sure there'll be other times." Liar.

"Oh, yeah, it'd be nice to see you."

"I'm sure you will," I said, "I'm sure you will." I'm so clever. "Well, I'll tell the old lady. I hope your mother feels better."

"She will. As soon as she finds out she spoiled our weekend. So long."

"Good-bye Joe."

I thought about Squillante as I twisted and packed the chop meat. Imagine, using your own mother as an excuse to skip town. If Sweetlips was telling the truth, that's what Squillante was doing. I decided to believe Squillante. Which made me disbelieve Sweetlips. Which made Saturday night a little more dangerous. Which kept me on my toes.

I ate my hamburgers.

By the time I got to Joe Cheese's establishment it was packed wall to wall with broads of all descriptions and men trying to make them. "Whattya givin' away?" I asked when I reached his table.

"Pussy," he laughed. "Wall to wall pussy." Thursday night, he explained, was always a good night because people who don't have dates for the weekend are out taking a good shot at getting one. And the more optimistic among them are trying to find a balling partner for the cold November night.

We talked about the general decline in morality for a few moments, both of us agreeing it was a good and wonderful thing, then we walked back into his office. "What we have heeereeeerrrrrr," he said, trying to imitate the jailer in *Cool Hand Luke,* "is one whole lot of money!" He handed me one package, wrapped in brown paper. I knew from past experience what was inside: two packages, each approximately three inches thick, of one-hundred dollar bills. "That is eighty-thousand dollars, my friend," he finished.

It wasn't necessary to count it. If the Cheese says a package contains a pound and a half of ostrich shit, you can be positive it is exactly one and one-half pounds, not an ounce more, not an ounce less.

"I'll see you next week."

When I come back to pay Joe Cheese his money, it would not be wrapped in neat little three-inch packages. The dealers I sell to pay with any denomination they can get their paws on, so there will usually be as many singles as hundreds. My wife and I sit up counting all night. It's really a funny scene; the entire dining room table is covered with green cash dollars and the two of us are packing bills into hundreds and thousands. When we finish I take some shopping bags and divide up shares: This is the Cheese's, this is mine, this is expenses. Joe's is obviously the biggest. The following night I pick up the shopping bag, or bags, filled with bills and covered with a newspaper, and walk into wherever we're meeting. The first time I did that Cheese went nuts. He couldn't believe anyone would treat money so casually. I wasn't worried: I knew I wasn't going to let anything happen to that cash.

My share of the profits can be anywhere from $2000 to $15,000, depending on the size of the load.

As I got up to leave Joe Cheese's establishment, he said, "Bring me a pack of Marlboros."

"Hard pack or soft?" I asked. When you're in the business you've got to be precise.

"Hard."

"It'll be my present." He walked me through the front door and wished me a good trip. Occasionally I would drive one of the trucks myself and he thought this was one of those times. I didn't bother to correct him. As far as I was concerned, the more people who thought I was out of town for the weekend the better it was.

I took the bundle of money and drove out to Jamaica, Queens, to meet Bobby Roach at the warehouse. This place was just a big empty building with garage-type doors. Certain individuals who were known to certain other individuals could rent space out and be sure no one was going to come snooping around. At various times all sorts of merchandise had been left there, much of it from temporarily borrowed trucks. When I got there our rented trucks were already inside.

The Roach was inside the cab of one with the two drivers trying to keep warm. I didn't feel comfortable at all inside the place. Because it was so empty every sound echoed a number of times, and the poor lighting cast shadows in every corner. It did not exactly present a feeling of security. "You guys all set?" I asked the drivers.

They nodded.

"You know the story. Do your job and there's a bonus at the end. Fuck with me or this money and you're dead. When do you think you'll be back?"

"It depends on how busy they are down there," one of them, an individual called Mack, obviously because he was a truck hauler, told me, "I'd say Saturday night, but don't be surprised if it's not until Sunday afternoon."

"No later," I said very seriously. I handed Mack the package. "There's eighty-thousand bucks there. It ain't my money, so guard it with your life." I knew he would, because he knew what I would do if the money disappeared. "Gentlemen, have a safe trip. Remember, thousands of smokers are depending on you guys."

After the trucks left Bobby and I walked out to my car. I asked him how the burglar-alarm business was going and he told me they were moving but slow. "You gonna be here Sunday?" he asked.

"I'm gonna try. I got some things to do over the weekend so I don't know how free I'll be during the day. I'll call you no matter what."

I left. The boards were clear. My bookmaking business was done for the week. The cigarette trip was on its way and I had nothing more to do. I was free and clear to deal with Squillante.

All I had to do was get a car and be at the spot early. I intended to be very early.

Although it was well after midnight when I got home my old lady was still up. "Where've you been?" she asked me, which is unusual for her. It's a question she very rarely asks.

"Sending out some trucks for a cigarette pickup." This is one operation I keep her well informed about. "Tell your girls they'll have their butts on Monday. Where you playing?"

She thought for a moment. "Patti's. I'll write down the address."

"Okay, I'll bring a van over there. Make sure they all bring their cars with them and I'll load them up." We talked for a few minutes, husband-and-wife small talk, and then she remembered to tell me we had been invited to my brother's house for dinner.

"When?" I asked.

"Saturday evening."

It figured. "I can't make it. I told you never to make plans for me without asking me first. You did it with the Squillantes and now you're doing it again. Don't you ever learn?"

Actually, she was pissed. "What do you mean you can't make it?"

I was starting to yell. "Don't you understand English? I can't make it. I got business."

"I'm not going to call your brother and tell him you can't make it."

"Good. I got a better idea. Call my brother and tell him we both can't make it."

"Don't tell me what to do. If I feel like going, I'm going."

I looked her right in the face and lowered my voice. "You ain't going," I said quietly. "I never tell you what to do. This time I'm telling you what to do. And you are staying right here, by yourself Saturday night."

She stopped yelling. She knew I was very serious. "Why? For what?"

"Because I said so, okay? I just want you here by yourself Saturday night because," I thought quickly, "because I'm expecting a very important telephone call and I can't be here."

"What am I," she screamed, "your answering service?"

"You are Saturday night. And if anyone calls, you tell them that I'm asleep inside." I wanted her there to establish an alibi in case I needed one. A wife is the perfect alibi. She can't be forced to testify against her husband, unless she volunteers, of course, and my old lady was not about to volunteer after all the money I had given her. She can, on the other hand, testify for the defense. And as long as she was home alone she would be in a perfect position to do so.

She was very quiet for a few minutes. She obviously knew something important was happening, but knew she couldn't ask about it. It was something unwritten between us, she never asked me about my work. In return she got just about everything her heart desired.

I broke the silence. "Joe Squillante called. They can't come Sunday night. His mother had a heart attack or something."

She didn't say anything. "Why don't you call my brother and tell him we can come Sunday night. Make up some story about Saturday night."

"Sometimes," she said quietly, "sometimes . . ." She didn't finish the sentence.

I was looking for something to say that would soothe her, because I really don't like to fight with her unless absolutely necessary. Finally I came up with the perfect answer.

"Wanna play some gin?" She did, and we sat up another two hours playing gin rummy. It worked out very well. She won $1.85 and went to bed happy.

RIGHT GUY,
WRONG CRIME

My wife was gone by the time I woke up Friday morning. I didn't know where she went, shopping with friends, to a movie, I didn't know. I just knew enough to be thankful for small blessings. I laid there in bed outlining the day. The only step still to be taken was getting an automobile, but that had to be after dark.

I got up and made myself some breakfast: two eggs over easy, a stack of wheatcakes and coffee with milk not cream. Then I opened the *New York Daily News* to my horoscope. It said Friday was a good day to meet new people "who have my best interests at heart," proving once again you can't believe everything you read.

There was a knock at my door around 11:30. I opened it and there stood the new people. Two of New York's finest, in full blue uniform. "Halloween was two weeks ago, kids," I said. I don't think they appreciated it.

"Are you ———?"

"If I ain't he's gonna be pissed when he gets home and finds I been sleeping with his wife." I really was in good humor. For some reason, though, they didn't laugh.

"Would you get dressed please, we'd like you to come downtown and answer a few questions."

"Do you have a warrant?" I always ask this question because it bugs the hell out of them. They admitted they didn't. "Don't worry about it fellows. Let me put a shirt on." What the hell, I didn't have any plans until much later anyway.

Actually that wasn't the reason I was so agreeable. Obviously they had some reason they wanted to talk to me, at this point I didn't know what, but deep in my heart of hearts I could only guess it had something to do with number 28. If I didn't cooperate they would have come back after me with a warrant. And that might have caused me real problems because I didn't know when they would serve it. If they caught me out in the street they would find a loaded .38 in my pocket, and that could cause more problems. So I was quite willing to go along with them.

I worry more about being caught for something silly, like carrying a concealed weapon, than getting picked up because of a hit. The hit I can do something about, the small things have a way of causing big trouble. Thus far I've been very lucky, but it's been close.

One night I had been doing an excess amount of drinking in Manhattan, and I don't believe in drinking and driving, so I grabbed a cab and asked the driver, "Feel like taking a ride to the Bronx?" I know cabbies don't like to go to the Bronx at night because they rarely can get a fare coming back into Manhattan and a cabbie can make more than the round-trip fare just by hanging around downtown. But this driver, an older guy in his late forties I would guess, said alright. He drove me home and we bullshitted along the way. When we got there I threw him a $20 bill and said thanks. He was most appreciative.

Two weeks later I was working on a contract. One evening I was walking down Madison Avenue a block or so behind my target. I looked across the street and I see the law in the person of two plainclothesmen who knew me very well. Unfortunately, I was carrying a piece on me at the time. Oh Jesus, I thought, now I'm fucked. I kept walking until I reached the end of the block and I had to stop because the light was just changing. Incredibly, the first car to stop at the light is my $20 cab driver. I took it as a message from heaven.

"Hey sweets," I said, "hold this for me," and in one swift motion took the cannon out and threw it on his front seat. "Ride around for a few minutes. If you come back and see me walking down the street, return it. If you don't I live at [I told him the address] and I'll be home later."

He nodded and drove off. I walked another block and sure enough the law stopped me. "What are you doing down here?" cop number one asked.

"Taking a leisurely stroll. Is that against the law?"

"Mind if I toss you?" cop number two asked.

"I mind," I said, "but go ahead and make yourself happy." He patted me down and amazingly enough didn't find anything.

"You know," number two said, "we don't like to see you down here. Why don't you stay up in the Bronx where you belong." It was a statement rather than a question.

"It's a free country pal, I can go wherever I want to."

Number one butted in. "We been watching you for six blocks. You been tailing that guy up ahead."

"What are you talking about? I had a heavy dinner and I'm walking it off. I told you, just a little stroll."

"If anything happens to him . . ."

I interrupted. "If anything happens to him what? What are you gonna do, come around and bother me? So you come around and bother me. Now if you got no further questions . . ." And I walked away.

I guess I walked about 20 blocks, up to 70th Street and here comes my friend in his cab. "You okay?"

I nodded and got in. "Let's go for a drive. Head over to the East River and get on the drive. I want to see if we have company." We didn't. I gave him $200 and my very best wishes.

I waited almost three months to hit the guy and, when I did, I did it in Brooklyn. I was a little itchy about making the hit, but once I had accepted the contract and the money there was no way I could back out of it. If you takes the money, you takes the chances. Actually, I didn't have that much to worry about. I felt pretty sure these detectives weren't going to the trouble of filing a report about our meeting. Policemen dislike filling out forms almost as much as burglars dislike policemen. Their real motive in approaching me, I'm pretty sure, was to make sure I did whatever I was going to do outside their precinct, outside all of Manhattan.

If I didn't, they would have to fill out more forms.

"You guys have any idea what this is all about?" I asked as we drove downtown. As soon as we headed toward Brooklyn I had no doubts about the subject: number 28. In my mind I began to go over each detail as best I could, and I began to formulate an alibi.

On that night, I began to recall, I spent the entire evening at home, by myself, reading the racing charts.

This is precisely the reason I don't like to take more than one hit within a two- or three-month period. Here I was busy with the police when I should have been thinking about stealing an automobile. And then it becomes difficult to remember which story is which.

We went to the 79th Precinct in Bedford-Stuyvesant. I thought this was a little peculiar because I haven't been near the 79th in five years.

The first thing they did when I got there was take me into a little room and read my constitutional rights to me. Then a detective I had never seen before walked in. "How are you, Joey?" he said.

I shrugged my shoulders. "You know, doin' alright."

"Glad to hear that. I had no doubts." He started looking over my sheet. "You've spent a lot of time in stationhouses, haven't you?"

In fact I had. I've been questioned in more than 20 murders, booked on one at this point, but never convicted. "Yeah," I agreed, "you people seem to think I'm something I'm not." I wondered when he was going to get around to 28.

"What you been doing lately?" He continued looking at the sheet while he spoke to me.

"A little of this, little of that. Nothing to concern yourself with."

"Of course not." He took a deep breath.

Here it comes, I thought, and braced myself so I would not react at all when he mentioned number 28's name.

"Joey, you ever hear of a guy named Carmine Alfano?"

I looked at him blankly.

"Maybe you heard of him by the name of 'Gimpy' O'Conner?"

"I never heard of the guy." It was no lie. I had never heard of him. He certainly was not number 28. Inside I was laughing. This was all just a bad coincidence. Some hood had been found not breathing and they had rounded up the usual bunch in hopes of finding something that might be useful.

They started asking me the usual questions and, since I knew I had absolutely nothing to do with this, I answered just as truthfully as I remembered. I was also polite and as witty as I could be. After about an hour of questions that led absolutely nowhere the detective tried to bluff me. "Would you like to call your lawyer?" he asked me.

Now, if I said yes, he knows that maybe I've got something I'm worried about. "I don't think so," I said, "unless you're going to book me. Otherwise, just keep askin'."

He smiled. He knew he was going to get absolutely nothing from me. "Okay, you can go home now. But stay around, allright." It wasn't a question.

"I'm not going anywhere," I answered, "and I'd like to take this opportunity to tell you it has been a real pleasure to be questioned by you." That was my one smart remark. I figured I could afford it, he had nothing on me.

Now I really had to start thinking about obtaining transportation for the activities of the morrow. There used to be a saying in my old neighborhood in the Bronx, "no wheels, no deals," meaning that without a car it was almost impossible to make money. By the time I was 15 I had my own automobile, even though I didn't have a license, and I practically lived in that thing. And throughout my career I've found that it is generally true: "no wheels, no deals."

Next to buying a car the easiest way to get one is to steal it. Actually, buying is harder, you gotta fill out all those goddam papers and invent addresses and stuff. I couldn't guess how many cars are stolen each year, but I know people who can get you any American car, in any color, within one week of your order. I, myself, would have to estimate that in my life I've stolen more than 100 cars. Some I've sold (when I lived in California I would take them down to Mexico), but most of them have been used in my deals. I've used stolen cars for everything from smuggling narcotics to making hits.

Actually there were a number of ways I could have gotten a car to use in the killing of Joseph Squillante. But I felt stealing one was the safest. I could have used my own, which is really stupid, I could have rented one, which is a little smarter but still dangerous because you have to sign things, or I could have gotten Jackie to get one for me. That much I didn't trust Jackie. I wanted a car that would work when I needed it to work. So stealing was best.

I only know of one individual who uses his own car in his work. He doesn't make hits, though, just robberies. He is an expert mechanic and has the thing so souped up that no police car could catch it on the open road. But in order to continue to use this car he is constantly painting it and changing license plates and matching registrations. That car must have been at least 15 different colors by now and he has a collection of at least 40 different sets of license plates and registrations. And, just to be on the super-safe side, when he registered it originally, he registered it to a vacant lot.

For me, it's not worth all the trouble. I don't have the needs of this guy. All I need is an automobile that will get me where I want to and get me away as fast as necessary. I don't bother with phony plates and registrations because, unless you're going to keep a stolen car more than three or four days, you have nothing to worry about. It takes that long for the coppers to get the plate numbers on their hot sheets. I had absolutely no intention of keeping the car that long; I was going to steal it Friday night, use it Saturday night when I burned Squillante, and then abandon it. I wasn't even going to drive it during daylight hours. So, could I go wrong? No way.

In fact, once I even stole a cab to use on a hit. I intended to park down the block from this guy's girlfriend's house and cruise by when he came out. I had watched him long enough to know he never, ever used his own car. And that's exactly what happened. I picked him up in the cab, drove three blocks and plugged him. The only difference in using a cab was that I had to take off all the inside handles, including the ones for the windows, and fix the locks so he couldn't operate them if he realized this was a setup. He didn't.

The other thing about that job that stands out is the fact that I made an extra $1.75. I took the cab on a Tuesday and, as I was driving up to the Bronx with it, I saw a guy hailing me. I had just heisted it and, with handles still in place, I picked him up, more as a joke than anything else. He was a film writer-producer on his way crosstown. The fare was $1.50 and he gave me a quarter tip. Don't knock it.

By the time the cops let me go home, I had dinner, argued with my wife and got ready to leave, it was dark outside. The only items I took with me were a pair of rubber surgical gloves and a few different lengths of wire. The gloves would keep my fingerprints off the car, the wire would enable me to break in and then get the thing started.

I knew exactly the type of car I was looking for. I wanted a dark colored, late model with absolutely no distinguishing characteristics like a short-wave antenna or a girl's name printed neatly on the side. I also knew the neighborhoods I was going to look around, neighborhoods in which the residents lived in buildings with limited parking facilities. That meant most people would have to park on the street wherever they could find a space. Very few people ever find spots close enough to their buildings to be able to look out a front window and check on their car. And, if someone else looked out and saw me fiddling with a strange car, you can lay odds they would bet it was just another sucker who left his keys in the ignition. It's 1000 to 1 they would even think about calling the police, much less actually do it. People just don't want to get involved, a fact for which I am always thankful.

I started my search in Manhattan. As I left my place I kept a very close watch for a tail; either the unknown Chevy or the police. I wasn't sure the police had quite finished with me. There was no way I was going to steal a car in the same borough I was going to make the hit. A simple case of super-caution. All I need is to be driving to make the hit and have the owner spot his car.

I drove around the Upper East Side of Manhattan for maybe 45 minutes without finding exactly what I wanted. I tried Queens next and found what I was looking for just off 108th Street. It was a dark green, 1966 Oldsmobile 98. A good, powerful car that had a reputation for being dependable. Once I found this car I had my next problem: finding a place to park my own car. One thing I didn't want was a ticket placing me in Queens and maybe connecting me with the car I was about to steal. I drove around the neighborhood at least a half-hour until I found a legal spot. It was about six blocks away from where my new Oldsmobile was parked.

I casually walked back and stood around for a few minutes just looking the situation over. It was very quiet. I put my skin-tight rubber gloves on, shoved the wire inside the rubber window lining and raised the latch. Once I'm inside, the car is as good as mine. All I have to do is open the hood and run a wire from the battery to the solenoid and the car will start. This is precisely what I did. The whole job took less than five minutes.

I've really never had any problems stealing cars because I'm careful and, when the situation calls for it, a good actor. I've only been bothered once, a passerby stopped and asked if he could help me. I played the angry car owner who had dropped his keys somewhere, "God knows fucking where," I grumbled, and let the schnook help me. That was the rare exception however. People really do mind their own business, with the rare exception of Mrs. Gibson.

Once I got the Oldsmobile started the first thing I did was check the gas tank. If the heap doesn't have at least enough gas in it to get me out of the area I'll turn off the engine, lock the door and leave. I do not want to take the chance of bringing my stolen car into the station where it is normally serviced and try to buy gas. There was a time I didn't let an empty gas tank bother me. When I was making a living stealing cars I would bring a siphon hose with me and, if the tank was low, just siphon enough gas to get out of the area from a nearby car. I never passed up an available Cadillac because it had no gas. Luckily, in this case, my unknown benefactor had the foresight to have three-quarters of a tank in our mutual engine. Enough to get me up to the North Bronx and a locksmith I do business with.

Locksmiths are God's gift to bad memories and good mobsters. A skillful locksmith can handle anything from a pair of handcuffs to a chastity belt. My particular need was a set of keys for the Olds, and I knew the perfect man to visit.

This particular individual, who will remain totally unidentified because he is still very much in business and unknown to the law, has been working with and for the organization at least 20 years I've known about. He is competent, dependable and quiet. All of which makes him expensive. He has his own house and car garage up in the North Bronx area and, because of the unusual hours kept by many of his clients, he was not at all unhappy about being awakened at half past two in the morning.

I pulled my car into his garage and watched him as he worked. He was truly a master craftsman. First he pulled the ignition out and checked the serial number. He asked me if I wanted a key made for the ignition that was in the car already, or if I wanted him to put in a new ignition switch. I told him to take his choice.

"Makes no difference," he said as he opened his workbox. This box was about three feet long and about a foot and a half high and contained some of the strangest tools I've ever seen. He checked some books he had against the make of car and ignition serial number, turned on one of his machines, and made the key for me right there. Then he did almost the same thing for the door. At this point I'm not sure if it was the same key or not, but I ended up with two keys, one for the door, the other for the ignition.

The price for the job was $100. It took 45 minutes.

While he was working on the key I checked the car over. I checked the battery, I checked the electrical system with my wire, I checked the tires. The only things that didn't work were the clock on the dashboard and the light inside the glove compartment, and I figured I could do without those. I checked the ignition and brakes while I was driving over and they were in good shape. So, generally, I was very satisfied with the car.

It isn't always that way. I've stolen cars that turned out to be pieces of crap and I've had to drop them on a corner. I certainly wasn't going to bring them back to where I found them. I have absolutely no hesitation about dropping a car if it doesn't feel right or perform well. All I have to do is go out and steal another one, and how difficult is that?

Once I had the keys my only small problem was finding a place to keep the car Saturday during the day. I found a 24-hour indoor garage and parked it up on the top level. Another $5.50 shot to hell. That done, the only large challenge remaining was to find a cab in the Bronx at 3:30 A.M.

Eventually I flagged a guy down and he asked his question before I got in the cab, "Where you going?"

I didn't answer him until I was safely inside the back. I figured the driver was not going to be too happy about going to Queens at that hour. But it was cold and late so I decided no more mister nice guy. "Queens," I said.

"Sorry," he snapped back, "I'm not going to Queens now."

Time to pull rank as a paying customer. "This sign you got here in the back says you got to take me wherever I want to go. Take me to Queens or I'll report you to the Taxi Commission." He agreed, although somewhat reluctantly. He dropped me off a few blocks from where I parked my car and I made the trip worth his while, paying him double what was on the meter. "See you in the Bronx," I said nicely as I got out of the cab.

"Anytime, bud," he now-pretty-happily replied.

I didn't feel like going right home. The first pangs of excitement were starting and I didn't want to go to sleep and lose them. I drove around haphazardly for a few minutes, just sorting my brain out. I wasn't sure exactly what was going to happen less than 24 hours later, but I had a reasonable idea. At 11 o'clock Squillante would show up. If this job was legitimate (even at this point I wasn't positive) I'd walk over to his car and blow his brains out. In theory that should be the end of it. But I expected more.

I tried to put myself in Jackie Sweetlips's head. If he was going to try to burn me, what would be the best way once he had me there? I came up with a few answers. Once I started walking toward Squillante's car I would be out in the open. If Squillante—or whoever was sitting in Squillante's car (they weren't above putting a ringer in the driver's seat)—was armed, and somebody moved in behind me, I'd be in the middle of a crossfire. There wasn't too much I could do about that except run like hell and duck. If that was the plan, I could wait in the park itself, and approach from the front of the car.

That would be fine, assuming Squillante showed up on time. It was simply too damn cold to stand outside and wait for him. If he was late I'd be frozen and my reflexes shot to hell.

The other possibility was even simpler. In this instance whoever was sitting in the car, Squillante or someone else—and this is assuming there is only one person in the car, who knows what's in a back seat—would be armed and as soon as I got near the car they would start shooting. About all I could do to prevent this was stay as close to the rear of the car as I could when I reached it, and as I moved to the side, stay as close to the side as possible. That would cut down on the shooting angle from inside the car considerably.

But as I thought about it, I realized that if this was a setup there simply wasn't a whole lot I could do about it except try to be lucky. I figured I would have the advantage of not being where I told Jackie I was going to be, and I intended to get there very early, and wait until after 11. These were all minor helps, but they were better than nothing.

It was after four in the morning when I decided to check the spot. I drove over and circled the block three times. It was a dark and desolate spot. I was the only car on the road.

I parked. Absolutely nothing happened. No dog walkers, no early risers, no cars driving through. The shadows played nicely across the area and filled the chosen spot with darkness.

I got out and walked around very briefly. There was a slight wind blowing and this I didn't mind, if there was a wind on Saturday night it would diffuse the pop the gun would make. I walked over to the rear door of the building and tried it. It opened easily and I walked in. The hallway was lit by a single lightbulb. I grabbed a garbage pail, which was sitting next to the rear staircase, and quietly brought it under the bulb. I climbed up on top and unscrewed the bulb. After I climbed down I opened the garbage pail and smashed the bulb. I didn't need any more light than nature provided.

When I left there I drove over to Squillante's building. There were no lights on in his apartment. I don't know what I expected to find, but I felt almost like the soldier on the eve of battle, like I did when I served in the Korean War, just standing and looking over the enemy encampment.

On the way home I stopped at a diner for a quick breakfast. Then I went home and slept soundly for the remainder of the night and into the middle of Saturday morning.

THE LONGEST DAY

Saturday turned out to be the coldest day of the fall. When I woke up the sky was a deep, dark, thunderstorm gray and it was obvious it was either going to rain or be the end of the world. I figured, rain for me, end of the world for Squillante.

Actually I didn't mind the bad weather. It would keep people inside and cut down on their vision.

The first thing I did was call Jackie Sweetlips. "I'll be by the lot in an hour," I said. "Will you be there?"

"I'll be there," he answered, "I got something you should know."

"What?"

"Not now. I told you, the walls have ears."

"I'll see you in an hour."

"Yeah."

Then I sat down with the *Daily News*. I like to catch up with what's happening in the city when I have the chance and the *News* is a good way to do this.

I don't remember there being much of interest in the paper that morning except the late betting lines for Sunday's pro games. I guessed that Squillante was probably doing the same thing I was doing, checking the lines, but I knew he wouldn't have to worry about losing his money. I hit a guy once who had a problem similar to Squillante's. He was a heavy bettor who had gotten deep into the hole and resorted to desperate means to get even. I hit him on a Sunday night—poof —he was gone. Here is the ironic part: I was told later Sunday had been his big day. He had bet seven or eight games and hit every one of them. Not enough to get even, but enough to bring him within screaming distance. I never did find out if the story was true or just street talk, to me it sounds like something someone would make up, but it's possible.

The day of a hit is not a very difficult day as long as you don't start worrying. If you're confident the day goes quickly. But if you spend the whole day worrying about what's going to happen and what problems you're going to have, you're just going to build yourself up into a bad nervous state, and then you will make your own problems. I was thinking about Squillante, but I was confident. And curious. I wanted to see exactly what Jackie had in mind for me this Saturday evening.

It wasn't always that way. The first few hits I made were somewhat difficult for this reason: I spent too much time thinking about them. The very first killing I did was as easy as pulling the trigger. I was 16 years old and working as a numbers controller. The job was offered to me by one of the people I worked for. The price was $5000, which is why I took it. The whole thing was simply a gut reaction. I got the offer, thought about it briefly, I put the bullet right where it was supposed to be put. Everything happened so quickly, from the time I was offered the job until it was finished, that I didn't have time to think of the consequences. I was so naïve I didn't know what they might be. Now I know, but I don't give a damn.

As I've said before, if I live, I live; if I die, I die. That's the way I am. I have done all those things I wanted to do. I have seen those things I've wanted to see. I am as complete a person as I'm ever going to be. In fact, there is only one piece of unfinished business to take care of: the man who tried to kill me and killed my first wife will be getting out of prison soon. When he does I'm going to kill him. But I think I said that before, didn't I?

Death does not faze me. Like Squillante, I'm going to die eventually. If I die a few years sooner, it's been a great life. And dying can't be all that bad—I've never heard anybody who did it complain.

The hits I was concerned with were the few I made after the first one, but before I had established myself as a complete hit man. I spent less time planning them and more time worrying about them. As I now know, it just isn't necessary to worry, good planning takes the worry out of the job. And when that planning is finished, I stop making changes, I just carry it out. If I was still running around trying to make changes on the very day I've planned to do the job, then I'm not qualified to do it.

Only on very rare occasions will a hit that has been well planned fail to come off. I tailed one individual for eight days before deciding where to zap him. According to the information I had been given he was a regular at a crap game in Queens, and I knew this to be a true fact because I had tailed him there twice. The crap game was a good spot because when he left he had to get in his car and drive over a steep hill at the top of the road. At the bottom of the hill was a very level, four-way stop, and there was no way he could avoid stopping there, no fucking way.

It was a perfect location. When I saw him come out

for his car I was going to race down the hill in my car and wait for him. I was going to be sitting in my car in the middle of the street, waiting at the stop sign. He would pull up behind me and stop. And wait. I was going to get out of my car like I had problems with it or I was mad at him for honking or something and walk right up to the window of his car and kill him.

The only problem was that he never showed up at the crap game. And it was very difficult to go ahead without him. I said to myself, what the fuck is this shit? I went over to his house, because I knew I could pick him up there, and I saw the place was tightly locked up. I spoke to the mailman and it turned out the guy had gone on vacation for a month. I blew my top, but there wasn't a thing I could do about it. I had to wait until he came back and start the entire tailing process all over again. It took another two and a half weeks, but I finally nailed him in a shopping-center parking lot.

I finished reading whatever there was to read in the news, bundled up tightly, and drove over to Jerome Avenue. Jackie came running out of his office shack and hopped into my car. "Cold enough for you?" he asked.

This is a question I always have an answer for. "No," I said, "I wish it was about ten degrees colder. My grandmother was an Eskimo." He looked at me and didn't know exactly how to react. Tough.

"Everything go alright?" I asked.

"Almost. But he'll be there. When he went to the bank yesterday I told him he was going to have something to do tonight. 'Fine,' he told me, 'I don't have any plans Saturday night anyway.' "

"He didn't seem edgy or nervous when you said that to him?"

"Not at all."

"That I don't understand. He should be ready to shit at anything unusual. I guess all guys are different."

Jackie backtracked when he saw me puzzled. "I don't know, maybe he did hesitate for a second. But when I told him there was some extra money involved he more or less jumped at the chance to earn."

I shook my head from side to side. Some men will do anything for money, I thought. "What'd you tell him?"

"Like we talked. He went for it, hook, line and sinker. I told him to be at Boston Road and 182nd Street, he said he knew where it was, at eleven P.M. and someone who was known to him, a friend, would come to him, get in the car and tell him where to drive."

"What'd you tell him about the individual he was supposed to finger?"

Sweetlips shook his head no. "Nothing. I said the guy would tell him about it while you were driving over. He believed."

"That's all?"

"He just wanted to know how many people were going to be there. When I told him one, he said okay."

There was only one detail missing. "Did you tell him to keep the door on the passenger side open?"

He snapped his fingers. "Sheet," he said, drawing it out, "I forgot. Listen, I'm sorry . . ." He's sorry and I'm going to be standing on a street in the Bronx with a loaded gun trying to get into a locked car. His apologies would not help open the door. This is precisely why I don't like to depend on other people for anything. When I do things myself they get done and they get done right. I guarantee you nobody cares about your own life as much as you do, so when you're putting it up for grabs you're smart to depend on the one and only. "You gonna see him?" I said.

Jackie was unhappy, naturally. At least he was putting on a good act. "I wasn't going to, but I guess I will. I'll drive over to the bank and meet him when he comes in. I'll tell him. Don't worry about it."

I looked him right in the eyes. "I worry about it," I said seriously.

"What should I tell him if he asks why?"

"How the fuck do I know? Tell him it's cold outside and I don't want to stand there while he fiddles around. Tell him anything you want. There's nothing unusual about a guy wanting to get in a car quickly. That should make him think it's not a hit. If it was a hit I could shoot him right through the window. Don't worry, he won't ask." I didn't know if he would or wouldn't, and I made a mental note to be ready in case the door was locked, as I expected it might be.

There were so many questions I wanted to ask Sweetlips as we sat there. He seemed quite at ease. I wonder how fast his tongue would have come out of his mouth if I asked him what he was doing leaving Squillante's place? I wonder how hard that tongue would have worked if I asked him who was trailing me? But I didn't ask. I didn't really need his answers. I would simply be ready for him. "Is he still packing to leave?" I asked.

Sweetlips made a face. "I guess."

"Don't you know?"

"How should I know?"

"Why the fuck don't you ask him?" I said sarcastically.

His tongue came shooting out of his mouth once again. "Don't start." It was meant as a threat and accepted as same.

"Relax, relax," I said. There was no reason to have it out here. "What was it you wanted to tell me?"

He got very dramatic all of a sudden. "Squillante just got himself a gun."

Piss. Shit. Fuck. I said as quietly and calmly as I could, "Nice of you to tell me. How'd you find out?"

"The punks told their contact yesterday. He told me last night."

"What kind of gun?" It didn't make any difference, a gun is a gun is a gun.

"An automatic. Is that gonna cause some trouble?"

I looked at him like he was the jerk he was. "It's not the best birthday present I ever had."

"Sorry."

"I'm sure you are."

This was a surprise. Not that Squillante was going to have a gun, I expected that, but that Jackie bothered to tell me about it. Even though the information sheet I had been given specifically mentioned he didn't own or use a gun, I would have been amazed if an individual in his circumstances wasn't carrying some protection every moment of the day.

But why did Sweetlips bring it up now? One possible answer came very quickly.

He said, "If you need some help, the Fat Man told me to tell you he'd supply whatever you wanted. He told me to do whatever you told me."

Now everything was getting a little clearer. This provided a perfect excuse for Sweetlips to be on the scene. I pointed a finger at his chest. "You just stay as far away from there as you can. I don't want to see you nowheres around there at all. Understand?"

"Yeah. Okay."

"It better be." I wasn't kidding. I had pretty much decided right then and there that if I saw Sweetlips that night I would kill him. "Now you just go tell Squillante what I told you." I paused. "Listen, if he gives you a problem tell him I don't want to get caught in the rain."

We drove back to the lot just as the rain was beginning. It rained on and off all afternoon.

As Jackie got out of the car I grabbed his arm. "And Jackie?"

"Yeah?"

"It's been real nice working with you." I said it just as sarcastically as I possibly could. He did not answer.

On the way home I thought about Joe Squillante and his gun. If that is all it is, Squillante and an automatic, I really wasn't worried. As long as I was quick he would never get to use it. People who don't normally handle guns are reluctant to shoot at all. And if you've never killed a man you're really going to take some time to think about it before pulling the trigger. I knew that no matter how scared Squillante was, when he saw it was me approaching the car, he would hesitate for a slight moment. He *thought* I was a hit man, but he didn't *know*. He simply couldn't be positive I was there to kill him. After all, I am a "friend." He would definitely take some time to think about what the Fat Man might do if he shot me and I was legit.

While he was thinking about it, I would kill him.

But I wondered if there was more to Jackie's conversation than that. He must have known I might assume Squillante was carrying a weapon. Particularly with what he was doing. Then why bother to tell me? One, to get on the premises. And two, I figured, to draw all my attention forward, to Squillante and his gun. That meant the attack would come from my rear, while my concentration was focused straight ahead.

Of course, there was always the possibility that Sweetlips was telling the complete and whole truth, and his words of warning were simply words of warning. He was, after all, responsible to the Fat Man that everything went off successfully. It was a possibility.

In any case, I thought back over the bag of tricks I've used, or heard of, that might be successful in situations like this one. One particular method edged into the corner of my mind. I figured it wouldn't be the whole answer, but it sure might help. I pulled over to a hardware store and went in.

It was pouring when I got home, so I pissed away a good portion of Saturday doing not very much of anything. I watched the college football games on the tube and I prepared to have an argument with my old lady. No way it was going to be avoided, and I wanted to get ready for it. One thing I did not want was to be really angry when I left the house. I didn't want to be in any emotional state. I wanted to be totally calm, totally relaxed, so I figured if I could get the fight over with early I would be in good shape.

I started the ball rolling about four o'clock. "You call my brother?"

She was late answering the bell for the first round. She didn't say a word.

I repeated myself. "I said, did you call . . ."

She came out in a defensive stance. "I heard you! Yes, I called there."

"And?"

She threw her first punch. "What do you care?" she jabbed. "You're not interested anyway."

I countered with a small jab of my own. "I told you, I got other things to do."

She met my jab with a roundhouse that missed.

"What could be more important than your own family? Your wife and your brother and your sister-in-law?"

I went into my peek-a-boo defense. "Leave me alone, huh. I told ya something, now just leave me alone with your nagging."

She tried a new offensive, something I hadn't seen her use in the ring before. "I'll leave you alone, I'll leave you alone. You can just bet on that."

I probed the new offense. "Now what is that supposed to mean?"

She really let loose with some shots to the head. "What does it sound like? Who do you think you are, telling me what to do all the time? I'll tell you something Joey, I've had it. I've had it. I don't want anymore of it. You don't own me."

I figured the best offense was a good defense. "Just what are you talking about?" I sneered.

She was definitely winning the round on points. "I think I've made myself quite clear."

"Not to me."

"Maybe if you listened to me a little more you'd understand what I was talking about sometimes. Okay, I'll spell it out. Tonight I'm going to stay here and if the phone rings I'm going to say you're asleep. That's tonight. But I don't know if I'm going to be here tomorrow or not."

I got in one final punch. "Suit yourself."

End of round one.

Round two was short and sweet. She was serving me a late-afternoon lunch when she asked, "What color is her hair?"

I laughed and countered. "Is that where you think I'm going? Is that it, huh? You're jealous? I told you, this is business I'm going on. Business."

She laughed. A weak counteroffensive.

I lowered my voice and looked at her straight on. "What do you think pays the rent on this place? What do you think buys your clothes and gas for your car and all those theater tickets and gifts for everyone from God to your mother? Where do you think that money comes from, huh?"

She didn't answer.

"Okay. Now you just sit here tonight and do what I ask you, okay? That's all I ask." Just to make sure I had a TKO I walked over and kissed her on the forehead. "You're my wife, and there is no one else in the world I care about."

It was true, even if I milked it a little for dramatic effect. I didn't want to do battle with a jealous wife. That can be true trouble. I knew of a hit man once who made a big play out of cheating on his wife. She fixed him—she hired a detective to tail him. And he tailed him right to a public hit. It ended their marriage, as well as the hit man's career.

On a ten-point scale, our fight rated a five. There weren't many punches, but the few that were landed were reasonably solid. I knew there would be more than one rematch.

She sat down with her needlepoint about 6:30. I stretched out on the couch, asked her to wake me at 8 P.M. and laid down to catch a quick nap.

When the alarm went off there was only one thought in my mind: Joseph Squillante. I just let him seep in until my body swelled with everything I knew about him. From this point on, until the job was done, Joe Squillante was going to be the center of my thinking. Everything I learned in the last weeks would be churning around in my mind, drawing a complete picture of what to expect when I started toward that car. By the time I left the relative safety of the apartment house and started that walk, my mind would have been through every eventuality numerous times.

This phase, this action phase, is obviously the most important—and most dangerous—part of any hit. This is where all planning is put to the supreme test and any mistakes will be magnified a hundred times. This is also where everything I had ever learned about killing would be called into play. There would be decisions to be made, decisions that would have to be made without time-consuming thought, decisions made simply by reaction.

Decisions that might mean the end of my life.

I splashed cold water on my face, more from habit than anything else, just to make sure I was completely awake. At about 8:30 I started getting ready. I don't have any special clothes I wear when I'm on a job— you wear the same thing too many times and you're liable to get yourself connected with a number of different jobs—but I do like to dress conservatively when doing heavyweight work. I picked out a pair of dark gray slacks and a plain, dark shirt. I would have liked to wear a sweater, but in case I had to get to my gun quickly the sweater might get in the way. The one concession I made to the cold was to bring a dark blue scarf my sister-in-law knitted for me. Dark socks, why not, and a pair of soft-soled shoes, the better not to be heard, or to slip on wet grass. I made sure I put on skin-tight gloves—to keep my fingerprints off everything. I topped it all off with a loose-fitting, dark lumber jacket. I own jackets that would have been warmer, but I wanted one I could move around easily in.

I took off my ring but left a plain, cheap watch

around my wrist. I wound it up and checked it against the kitchen clock, which runs on Old Lady Time—15 minutes fast so my wife won't be late for any appointments.

In general I looked very normal, which is precisely what I wanted. This is how you really dress to kill. The idea is not to look too conspicuous, but also not to look too inconspicuous either. In actuality, I would never wear these particular pants and that particular shirt together, because they really don't match. But I wasn't going to the senior prom.

The last thing I did before leaving the house was check my arsenal. Because I didn't want to make it obvious to my wife what I was doing, I picked up my weapons while she was out of the bedroom and locked myself in the bathroom. I planned to carry three weapons with me: the new .38 which I would actually use on Squillante; the .38 I always carry in case I ended up in a situation where I needed extra firepower; and my miniature shotgun, in case I had to shoot quickly and hit something 30 feet away. It might just give me enough extra time to aim the .38. I loaded all the guns in the bathroom. At one time I would wait until I was actually at the location before loading, but then I heard a scary story about a hit man I once knew. He worked just like I did, loading at the scene of the crime-to-be. Unfortunately, one night he started loading and the bullets fell right through the chamber. He had grabbed the wrong ammunition, and blew the job. So I load before I leave.

I filled one pocket with about a dozen extra shells and stuck the silencer in the other pocket, picked up the flashlight and checked its batteries, took a good long piss, grabbed my rubber gloves and left my apartment about a quarter of nine.

"What time will you be home?" my wife asked, sounding more curious than concerned.

"Late," I said.

"What does that mean?"

I shrugged my shoulders. "When I get done I'll be home."

She turned her back and walked away from me. "Don't wake me when you come home." That was the least I could promise her.

Under normal circumstances I would have taken a cab to the garage to pick up my borrowed car. But it was still raining pretty hard, and the forecast called for more rain, so I decided to take my own car. With the rain it might be tough to get a cab when I needed one. I don't like the additional worry about where I left my own car. Although I've never heard of it happening, I wouldn't want to have New York City's finest tow my car away because I parked near a hydrant while I was making a killing. In this case I was planning to leave my car in the 24-hour garage.

As I drove over I wondered exactly what Squillante was doing. I assumed he was probably just finishing his last supper.

I put my rubber gloves on before I got near the stolen car. Its engine turned right over. The gas tank read almost full, but I made a quick stop to top off the tank anyway. Seventy-eight cents worth of high test. I'm glad I didn't ask the attendant to clean the windshield.

It took me about 25 minutes to get over to 182nd Street and Boston Road from my house. Normally it's a shorter trip, but I was going very slowly. When I got there I drove as if I was just passing through. I looked around and saw nothing extraordinary. Then I drove through again. And a third time. It looked very peaceful, very quiet.

I turned the car around and came back in the other direction. Again, peaceful and quiet. I parked the car and sat there for a few moments, just looking around. The rain had stopped and the water made the streets shine as if they had just been scrubbed clean, leaving little puddles here and there. It was cold and there didn't seem to be a single person on the streets. I was totally alone.

It was a perfect night for killing.

BUT FIRST A BRIEF WORD
FROM MY SPONSOR

I waited.

And I started thinking. About Squillante. About Sweetlips. About the next two hours. Like a boxer in the last few moments before walking into the ring, or football players huddled in the locker room before kickoff, I mentally prepared myself for killing Joseph Squillante.

I can kill a man with absolutely no remorse, but I have to build myself into a certain emotional state to do it. I never really understood that until recently, when I started trying to analyze how I can do what I do without any feeling, when I started trying to understand what kind of person I am.

I know it is unusual to be able to work like this and the reason I can do these things, I believe, is that there is a lot of fuckin' hatred inside me for these people that I work with every day. People like Sweetlips. That may come as a surprise, but I think it's very true. Even though I associate with them, I laugh with them, I go with them, deep inside I hate them. I hate them not because of what they done to me, but because of what they did to my first wife. Many people can't accept the fact that, basically, I am not a bad individual. I am not an evil person. I like most people I come in contact with.

But I have learned one thing. When you kill somebody, you've really got to hate them. So, subconsciously, I guess when I'm pulling the trigger, what I'm really doing is killing the people who killed my first wife all over again. Killing these people . . . it just doesn't faze me. And Squillante was one of these people, no matter how well he dressed or how polite he was.

As I sat there, building emotion, all this subconsciously raced through my mind. The surface was calm. I felt very ready.

I parked the car, as I told Sweetlips I was going to do, approximately 20 yards from where I expected Squillante to park, and in a spot where I could watch it from the back door of the apartment house.

After I checked my weapons one more time to make sure they were as ready as I was, I got out of the car and started walking through the area. I walked very casually, looking around, taking in everything. The excitement, that sort of intensity, kept growing inside me. No matter how many hits you make, and this was going to be the 29th time I pulled the trigger, there is an incredible feeling of power that surges through you. I was beginning to feel its growth as I walked and waited for Squillante to arrive.

I knew he would be there on time. You can always depend on numbers controllers to be prompt. They have to be because they usually have so many places to cover that if they miss one meeting they throw their entire schedule off. So being on time gets to be a habit. Although I didn't know for sure where he was coming from, my guess was that it would be from his own apartment. In that case, at 10:15 I figured he was just getting into his car to drive on over.

I didn't see anything of great interest in the area. One thing I was particularly looking for was anybody who looked like he might be a friend of Squillante's, or an employee of Sweetlips's. But there just didn't seem to be anyone there at all.

I thought about Sweetlips. He knew I would be arriving at the spot early. If he was going to hit me this evening he would have to be getting there soon himself.

Finally I walked over to the apartment building. As expected, it was open. The bulb had not been replaced and so the hall was dark. I stepped inside and stood watch, out of the cold. It was 10:25.

I was watching everything. The exhilaration was growing. It is almost sexual, like one huge orgasm. Just growing and growing until it all lets loose. Within me I know I am playing judge, jury, executioner and God. I felt like I was 15 feet off the ground and I was doing my best to contain it, to control it, to keep my senses sharp and alert. But it is difficult. In a situation like this you are aware that, for one individual, you are heaven and hell, you are the ultimate.

The adrenaline just flowed right through my whole body, putting me in a super-sensitive state. I was attuned to everything. I was completely and totally aware of everything around me, every sound, every smell, every slight movement of a leaf. I could hear sounds the average person can't hear and that ordinarily I couldn't hear. There is a point at which thinking ceases and movement and reaction begins. I was building toward that point.

And I waited. And it grew. The thoughts I had were

fleeting and disconnected. I thought of my first wife and I let that build inside me. I thought of my weapon, this beautiful piece of precision machinery, and exactly what would happen when I pulled the trigger. In a microsecond all the moving parts would mesh together to push a solid piece of metal forward and into Squillante's skull. The supreme result of the industrialization of the world. It seemed a magnificent thought.

Slowly all of these faded and my mind began the blanking-out process. If a human being can go back through the ages and bring back all his animal instincts, it is at a time like this. There are no thoughts of business or duty, or money or a job, I was past all that. Now it was the most basic of all: survival of the fittest. Me.

This phase builds to a peak and then, then it begins to fade. Thoughts come back and you settle into a middle ground, half-thinking, half-reacting. The perfect time to pull the trigger.

At 19 minutes before 11 a car came down 182nd Street and slowed down. As it passed by my car it slowed almost to a stop and then continued up Boston Road. It went another 15 yards or so, just out of my vision through the door, and stopped.

I opened the door slightly so I could see what the car was doing.

Nothing. The driver was just sitting there. It was not Squillante and, in the dark, I could not distinguish exactly who it was. Carefully and silently I slid out of the door and, moving quickly and keeping my back against the building, I slid toward my car.

I reached into my belt and pulled out the new .38 as the driver's door opened and an individual hopped out and began walking toward my car. I reached into my jacket pocket, pulled out the silencer, and screwed it on. As he had opened the door the interior light of the car went on for a brief second. Long enough for me to recognize this not-so-unexpected visitor.

Jackie Sweetlips had come to say good-bye.

I stood silently as he walked toward my car. Immediately I knew what he expected to find: my body slumped in my car. Evidently his killer was supposed to be there before me and have done the work by now. I waited to see his reaction when he realized I wasn't dead in that car.

As he came closer to the car he put his hands up, almost in a gesture of surrender. This puzzled me. He walked to the car and peered in. In one quick, abrupt motion he jerked his head up. He knew I was alive and, at that moment, I'm sure he knew I had him dead in the sights of my weapon.

He stepped back from the car, but didn't start to retreat. Instead he looked around, slowly at first, but then faster and faster. I moved down the building even closer to him, keeping my body against the darkened wall and making no sound. By the time I reached the corner of the building I was no more than eight yards from the car. But he was standing on the other side, in the street, a mass of Detroit steel between him and me. I could do absolutely nothing but wait silently. I felt supremely confident. Whatever his plan had been, it had not worked. I was alive and about to destroy him.

He put his hands in his pockets and began moving toward the rear of the car. I picked a spot about five feet behind the car. When he reached that spot I would blast him.

He walked slowly and casually, not seeming to be in any great hurry, yet obviously nervous. He continued moving his head from side to side, then rocking on his heels and turning around to see if I was moving in behind him. He moved closer to my spot.

I switched the safety off the gun and leveled it. He was still moving.

Suddenly, and unexpectedly, he stopped. Then in a low, very urgent voice, looking off into the park where he obviously thought I was hiding, he called "Joey! Joey, where the fuck are you?" It saved his life.

Staying completely in the dark I called back, also in a low monotone, "Get your hands straight up in the air and walk into the middle of the street." In the silence our voices sounded very loud.

As he moved away from the car, hands held high in the air, I darted out behind him and grabbed the neck of his coat by the collar. I almost threw him across the hood of the car.

"Hey! Take it . . ."

I stuck the gun right at his temple. "I'm gonna give you ten seconds to save your life. If you don't have a super-reason for being here, you're dead."

He started to stand up. "What the fu . . ."

I pushed him back down. "Ten. Nine." I wasn't kidding. I had no doubts he was there to kill me and I wasn't about to give him the chance. As I started counting I took a quick glance behind me. I didn't want anyone sneaking up on me while I was holding Sweetlips.

"Lemme turn around, will ya. Ease up Joey. What are you, crazy? I'm not the guy . . ."

I realized he was right, he couldn't talk with his mouth being pushed into the hood of the car. I let him stand up, but not turn around. "You got six. Five."

He rubbed the back of his neck. I couldn't see his mouth, but I could guess that his tongue was working furiously. "I came to tell you Squillante is bringing help with him tonight."

I stopped counting. "Go on."

"One of the two hoods who were doing his stick-ups reported in to me today and said that Squillante hired him for a job tonight."

The cold air turned our breath into puffs of white smoke as we spoke. Sweetlips was really scared, I could hear it in his breathing.

"Whattya mean?" I demanded.

"Whattya mean, whatta I mean? I mean just like I said. Squillante told them to get guns because they were driving back-up to a meeting he had to go to."

It made sense. It was a smart precaution. Things had been too easy for Squillante not to have some sort of emergency system planned. I *knew* he couldn't be that stupid.

"Why the fuck didn't you get in contact with me?" I asked.

"I tried," he said, "I tried. I been calling Petey all fuckin' afternoon and evening to contact you. I couldn't get in touch with him and I don't know how the fuck to reach you. So I came here myself."

I didn't know whether to believe him or not. There were a whole bunch of unanswered questions that seemed to form a picture. Now he was telling me it was the wrong picture.

"What about the cab driver?" I asked him.

"What cab driver? What are you talkin' about?"

"Don't fuck with me baby," I warned, "because the safest thing for me to do right now would be to make holes in you." It was, and I was really tempted. "You know what cab driver. The fuckin' guy you had try to run me down, that's what cab driver."

"Run you down? Hey, Joey, you're seeing shadows.

When I settle with somebody, I do it myself, I don't hire muscle to settle personal beefs."

For an individual whose life was hanging by a thread he was doing a good job answering the questions. He was keeping himself alive, but I still wasn't sure if he was leveling. I didn't know what to do, but I knew I had to do it quickly. Squillante was due any minute and all I needed was to have him drive up and see me standing there holding a gun on Sweetlips. He wouldn't stop running until he was so safe even his mother couldn't find him. So I decided I'd better move. With Sweetlips.

"Turn around, but keep your hands up high." He turned around and I patted him down quickly.

"Go ahead, look," he said, "I ain't even packing a weapon." He wasn't. All of a sudden he seemed to realize something. "Hey, what is this? You don't think . . ."

I stopped him. "Look Sweetlips. I don't like you. You don't like me. You been threatening to get even with me for a long time."

He laughed cautiously. "And you thought?"

"I still think," I said. We understood each other completely. I was running a hundred things through my head just as quickly as I could. If Squillante didn't show I would know Sweetlips was lying about the entire project. Then I would definitely have to kill him. "Take your belt off," I told him.

"My pants'll fall down," he started protesting.

"OFF!" I wasn't in any mood to argue. I took his belt and tied his hands behind his back just as tightly as I could. It wasn't a very strong bond, but he would not be able to move quickly with the belt on. That would give me extra time. "Move," I prodded. We walked over to his car and turned it off. I took the keys and put them in my pocket. I wasn't worried about leaving the car there, Squillante would never know it was not supposed to be there.

"Let me tell you something. When the Fat Man hears . . ."

"Shut up. Just move." I pushed him to the rear of the building and brought him into the hallway with me. "Sit down!"

"It's fuckin' wet."

I pushed him down. Then I leaned over and pointed the gun right between his eyes. His tongue was wearing away his lips. "I got some questions," I said quietly, "and you better have some answers. Who's been tailing me when I picked up on Squillante?"

"The two hoods. They told me tonight. Squillante has been having them tail him for over a week. They picked you up, but they told Squillante it wasn't a tail, just a coincidence."

"Why'd they tell him that?"

He seemed to be gaining some control over his fear. His only problem was that the muddy water on the floor was spreading over his pants. "Joey," he pleaded, "don't you understand? Those guys are working for us now. The Fat Man scared the shit out of them. They know that when Squillante's dead they'll go free. They ain't gonna help him."

I kept remembering that Sweetlips was talking for his life. If his answers weren't good, I would kill him right there. We both knew that.

And, even if his answers were good, if I had the slightest doubt, I would still have to kill him. "Didn't you know they were tailing me?"

"No, Joey, I swear to Christ I only just found out today. They said they didn't tell me before because they didn't think it was important. Okay, they're stupid. Then this meeting thing and the guns came up. They got scared and called me."

"That's beautiful," I said, "that's wonderful. There's only one problem, jerk. These guys were tailing me when I was driving my own car. They got my license-plate number. They can tag me if they want to. What are we gonna do about that, huh?"

"Believe me, Joey," he said, "believe me, they won't tag you."

"Why not? How come you're so sure?"

A lot of peoples' lives, the hoods', Sweetlips's, even Squillante's, depended on this answer. If it wasn't good enough, I would have to put off hitting Squillante to another time, another place. "It's simple," Sweetlips explained, "they got nothin' to gain and their lives to lose if they turn you in. They know the police won't kill them if they don't answer their questions—and they know the Fat Man will if they do."

It made a lot of sense. The hoods might be stupid, but they seemed to like living. My real problem was Jackie Sweetlips. The safest thing to do would be to kill him. I could always find something to tell the Fat Man. After all he was on the killing ground, and there was no reason except he fucked up.

But then I had another thought. If he was up-and-up with me, Sweetlips had come out here, at the risk of his own life, to help me. I didn't understand that, so I asked him about it.

"Believe me, it ain't for you," he said. "I couldn't care less if you live or die and if I had a preference you know which way I'd go. But I got a job to do and that is to make sure Squillante's dead. The Fat Man wanted you and I got you. So I gotta follow through on it. Believe me, when I tell you it ain't for you."

There was still one major question bothering me. I

wanted to hold onto it, to pop it at a better time, at a time when I could read the truth from his reaction, but there was no better time. It was almost 11 and Squillante would be coming around the block any minute. So I asked. "Here's the big one, Jackie. You answer this and I may believe you. What the fuck were you doing at Squillante's apartment the other night?"

He didn't even pause. "I was doin' the guy a favor! His mother had a heart attack and he couldn't get over to the bank and to the hospital in time for visiting hours. He was trying to balance his schedule and I was dropping off his lists and his payoffs. That's all, it's my job."

I believed him. I wouldn't swear by him, but I believed him. That was enough to prevent me from killing him. But now the problem became Squillante. There was no way I could kill him with witnesses around, even if they were in the Fat Man's debt. If they saw me killing Squillante they would have to go too, and two more killings were hassles I didn't need. The police aren't going to bother too much when one hood gets killed. When three get it, it's sort of a massacre and there are problems. "Well, Jackie, ole' buddy," I said sarcastically, "what do we do now?"

"Whattya mean? You gotta kill him."

"I don't gotta do shit. What happens if I don't?"

"You're gonna lose him. He's leaving Monday on an eleven o'clock flight to Europe. A one-way ticket."

"What about his mother?" What a dumb question. "What about his own life?"

I asked him if he thought Squillante suspected something. He nodded. "I'm sure he suspects now. I didn't think so when I spoke to you this morning, but he's doin' too much for a guy who thinks he's in the clear."

I remembered an old saying: Even the best laid plans go awry. I really had no choice but to go ahead and kill Squillante, but there was no way I could follow my original plan. I started trying to work something out in my head, something quick and easy. One thing was obvious, it wasn't going to be here, not with his two sheepdogs following him. They had to go. I made a very dangerous decision, the first time in my career I ever found myself in this bind, I was just going to play it by ear.

I had one advantage that might make the difference: I knew I was going to kill him; he could only suspect it.

Sweetlips just sat quietly on the floor. I think he understood that I was really working in my head. I checked my watch. It was just after 11. "Let me tell you something babe," I said to Sweetlips, without taking my eyes away from the window, "what you say sounds good and I think I believe you. But if Squillante don't show up, all I can figure is that this was a setup." I looked at him very quickly. "And then I'm going to kill you."

One minute passed.

A second minute passed. No movement on the street.

It was 11:06. Sweetlips was getting a little nervous. I could hear him twisting the belt. I decided I'd better check it out and leaned down behind him to tighten the notch.

As I did I heard a car outside. The Chevy sedan, two men in front, drove by slowly. If Jackie was right, Squillante would follow and these boys would circle the block and pull up somewhere behind him. Two minutes later Joseph Squillante pulled into the space he had been directed to. Sweetlips started breathing easily again.

Squillante left the engine running as he sat there. He was simply looking over the area. Evidently he was satisfied because he turned the car engine off, then turned the lights out.

The dim streetlight down the block cast weird shadows from the tree branches and barely lit up the inside of the car. I could see Squillante lean across the front seat and open the latch on the passenger side. Then he clasped his hands behind his head and stretched. He released, leaned back, and began waiting.

I watched him. And I waited too. I had no doubts that sitting next to him on the front seat was his new gun. If he was totally petrified I was in trouble. As soon as he saw me he'd start shooting. Knowing this, I stood quietly inside, giving him some time to relax, to let the tension ease up. Giving him time to get used to his surroundings. The peace and quiet of the place.

I was not at all comfortable. I stood inside the doorway, hands at my side, just watching him and the area. His eyes, I'm sure, shifted more than once to the rear-view mirror. And we waited. For what, I don't know, the perfect moment, the moment when the man on the high diving board finally feels completely and totally ready. Soon.

So far the hoods didn't seem to be back. I was watching for the lights of their car on the rear of Squillante's bumper, because I couldn't see back down the block, but so far they didn't seem to have come back. I was suspicious of everything else in the area. If the wind started to blow I would be suspicious. Why did the wind suddenly start to blow? Is there any law around waiting for me to make my move? Are there any honest citizens in the area? I waited some more.

211

Jackie sat wet and quiet, not saying a word. In the back of my mind I understood the possibility that Sweetlips had sweet-talked me into a trap, that when I was halfway to Squillante's car his hired guns might open up on me. There was only one way to find out, but I wasn't quite ready.

At almost 11:30 I took a deep breath, checked my silencer to make sure it hadn't loosened, and started to move to open the door. But just as I did, Squillante started moving around in his car. I stood motionless. There was no way he could know where I was coming from, but I didn't know what he was up to. All of a sudden, his door opened and he stepped out of his car. I scrambled back away from the door, a reflex action because I knew he couldn't see me, and waited for what he was going to do. This was another of those totally unexpected events which seemed to be plaguing this entire hit.

In all the jobs I've done, this was the first time somebody had done something quite as unexpected as Squillante was doing.

He looked around the area very slowly and then, just as slowly and carefully, he walked to the front of his car and stood motionless. Now I knew. I couldn't actually see what it was but I had no doubts. Joseph Squillante was taking his last piss.

Inside, I laughed. I was more relieved than he was. Who knew what that crazy fucker would do? Take a piss. Actually, Squillante was lucky, taking a piss is a luxury to a hit man. If I've got my duck sitting and I'm waiting for the moment and I've got to take a piss, I've got no choice but to go in my pants. And taking a shit is completely out of the question. On the day of a hit I'm very, very careful about what I eat. No bananas, no beans, no prunes or prune juice and very little fruit. Nothing that is going to make me shit.

Squillante finished and walked back to the side of the car. Again he looked around and stretched, and then he took his jacket off. He threw the coat across the front seat. I squinted as best I could and there, shoved into his belt, was the gun. He stood there, leaning against his car, waiting.

It didn't strike me then, and only now as I remember that night do I think of it, but Squillante must truly have been very frightened. That was one cold night, he had turned the engine off, and yet he was still sweating enough heat to take his jacket off.

I watched him standing out in the cold, alone, looking around, and I began to get a little itchy. He wasn't doing anything at all except standing there. Under my breath I muttered something like, "Get back in the car you motherfucker."

"What?" Sweetlips whispered.

"Shut up," I whispered. It was a command.

I waited because there was no way I was going to expose myself while he was standing outside. That gave him too much mobility. I wanted him in the front seat of that car, trapped like a rat. Finally, finally he climbed back into the car as the cold reached him. Now I had him just the way I wanted.

I reached into my belt and hoisted the new .38 into the air. Then I gently stuck it back in my pants, keeping my hand on the handle. I checked to see that I hadn't put the safety back on. I hadn't.

I pulled my old .38 from its leg holster. I took the safety off and put it back.

I reached into my pocket and pulled out the flashlight. Bending very close to the ground, so there would be no reflection at all, I turned it on and off quickly. It worked perfectly.

Finally I reached into my pants pocket and pulled out Jackie's car keys. I threw them on the ground next to him. I took one deep breath, checked the new .38 one more time, pushed open the door and started walking toward the car. "What about . . ." Sweetlips started to whisper.

I knew he could free himself in a reasonable period of time. "Freeze," I said, and left him sitting in the cold.

THE LONGEST NIGHT

I started walking toward the car. Slowly at first, then I speeded up just a bit. The total distance between the building and Squillante's car was no more than 30 yards, a distance I can normally cover easily in less than 30 seconds. I have no idea how long it took me that night, but it was quite a bit longer.

Jackie Sweetlips, left sitting in a puddle inside the hallway, was forgotten, a part of my distant past. Everything was now, this moment.

Mentally I divided the 30 yards into three separate areas of concentration. The first ten yards I looked to my sides and behind me, trying to locate either the Chevy with the two punks in it, or pick up anybody that might be coming up on me from the rear. I couldn't find the Chevy, and I began to think the hoods just took off. There didn't seem to be any other movement behind me.

I walked right into a big puddle I never even noticed. My shoes and socks soaked right through and I knew this was going to add to my unhappiness.

I spent the second ten yards surveying the area in front of me. I made visual arcs, as I learned in the army, each arc just a bit wider and deeper than the one before it. If anyone was going to come out of the park toward me I wanted to pick him up very quickly.

The last ten yards were all Squillante's. I walked toward the car at a steady pace. I was not in any hurry to get there. I had absolutely no idea what was going through his mind as I made this walk. I had to assume he was scared. Scared to be there, scared to be meeting somebody, scared to be holding a loaded gun in his hand.

I had no doubts he was holding the gun and ready to use it. I just wanted to make sure I could startle him briefly. That would at least prevent him from shooting on sight. If he did that I didn't have a super-wonderful chance of walking away unhurt.

I reached my left hand into my belt and pulled the new .38 free. I kept it inside my coat, completely concealed. I took one quick look over my shoulder, again trying to pick up the Chevy. If they weren't there, I could simply blast him and walk away. If they were there, they were watching me make this walk. I already know they can't stand up to pressure—they talked quick enough when the Fat Man asked the questions—so I know they're going to talk if some high-powered detective is doing the asking. I could not afford any witnesses.

Squillante realized I was coming when I was approximately ten yards from the car. I could see him watching the rear-view mirror at that distance and, as I got closer, he shifted his body so he was facing the passenger door. I knew his gun was sitting in his hand.

I made sure I stayed as close to the car as I could. When I was briefly hidden by the dead visual spot between the back window and the rear side window on the right side of the car, I stuck my right arm as far away from my body as I could, pointed the flashlight

216

right where I guessed Squillante's head was going to be, and turned the beam on.

There was no shot. I eased up a little on my breathing. Normally if an individual is in a state of panic and a light goes on quickly and unexpectedly, he'll fire away at it. As long as my body isn't behind it, I won't get too badly hurt. And the beam from the light will cause him to become temporarily blinded, making him an easy target.

But he didn't fire. I reached the car and opened the door very wide. As I thought, he was holding his gun in his right hand, pointing it more or less in my direction.

"Whattya say, Joe?" I said as calmly as I could, then slid into the passenger seat. It'd been a long time since I was looking down a gun barrel first.

He looked at me almost blankly. He knew who I was, yet didn't know what to make of my being there. He *knew* I was a hit man, but he didn't know if I was there to hit him. So he did nothing. He sat and kept that thing pointed right at me.

Moving very easily so as not to upset him, I took my right hand and pushed the gun away from me. "Watch it," I said, "those things hurt people when they go off." I also took my left hand off my gun, but left the .38 loose inside my jacket, so I could get at it very quickly.

He seemed to come out of the daze. "Hey Joey," he said almost brightly, "I didn't expect to see you here."

I agreed. "Yeah, it's sort of a surprise party."

He still didn't know whether to believe that he was the intended or not. If it had been me sitting in his seat I would have plugged me as full of holes as there were bullets available. But he wasn't used to the gun, so he hesitated, and hesitated. "Who's gonna be surprised?" he asked.

What was I gonna tell him? "You'll see," I finally answered. Then I sort of gave him a command. "Listen, put that thing away and let's go."

"Where?"

"Just drive, I'll tell you where." I think I finally got through to him. He put the gun inside his belt and turned frontwards. He started the car.

"What's with the flashlight?" he asked as naturally as he could, but still with some strain.

"It's dark out. I wanted to make sure it was you in this car." I paused for effect. "What's with the gun?"

He tried to be casual about it. "Oh, you know. It's dark, it's late, I didn't know who I was meeting. And . . . well, I've had some problems with some people and I just wasn't sure that you weren't one of them."

"Problems?" I asked, as if I didn't know.

He did not elaborate. "Problems," he said. As he started to back the car up I took a good long look in the rear-view mirror. About 40 yards behind us a pair of headlights flashed on and off, then stayed on. The boys of night had indeed returned.

In my mind I was trying to figure out two problems: one, how to drop the tail and two, where to take him. "Just head downtown," I told him, I knew I'd come up with something. I also knew it shouldn't be too difficult to lose a tail that didn't want to stay attached. The hoods knew that the Fat Man held their lives in his hand, so I knew they weren't going to be too serious about tailing Squillante, especially after it became obvious he was trying to lose them. I just had to give Squillante a reason to want to lose them. They had done their job—they had gotten Squillante to his appointment.

"Yeah," I said as easily and friendly as I could, trying to set something up, "I know what you mean about problems. I got problems too. That's the real reason for the flashlight."

"What sort of problems did you have?"

"Just problems," I said. We both laughed. I think he was beginning to feel more comfortable with me.

We rode silently down through the Bronx as I tried to figure a location Squillante would find believable. My first choice was under the Williamsburg Bridge, where I first met with Petey, but I knew Joe would never go for that. He's supposed to point somebody out, that's the story, and I knew he wouldn't expect to find a crowd under the bridge at midnight.

Where would he find a crowd? The answer was obvious: at a restaurant. Outside a restaurant would be okay. In a big parking lot. In the back of a big parking lot. I started to think of restaurants I knew in Brooklyn or Queens with big parking lots. Then I thought of one. A big place in Queens, right on the water. "When you reach the Fifty-ninth Street Bridge," I told him, "take it to Northern Boulevard."

He nodded.

I was trying to make small talk. Now that I knew the spot, I wanted to get rid of the tail. How? "How's your mother doin'?"

"Better," he said. "The doctor said it wasn't a heart attack really, just a warning."

"That's scary enough," I said.

He agreed. "You know, Joey," he said after a pause, "we really haven't been that friendly over the years, but I'm glad it was you out there tonight. I have to tell you something. I was nervous as hell sitting there.

I really thought it was a setup. I felt better when I saw it was you."

These were all nice words, but I knew they were bullshit. If he felt so good about seeing me he would have released the tail. He was trying to lead me into some sort of corner. "Yeah, well, I was glad when Jackie told me it was you who was gonna be here tonight, too," I agreed.

I leaned forward and looked in the mirror. "Listen babe," I said, "I don't want to scare you or anything, but I think we got company."

He made a big show of leaning over and looking in the mirror. "You sure?"

"No, not exactly. It's just that there's a car that's been right behind us the whole trip."

"I doubt they're following us."

"Not us," I said, "me. I told you I had some problems. Well, I think somebody is trying to solve them tonight."

Squillante simply did not know what to do. He couldn't admit that the boys on his tail were his because this was a legitimate job for him and he could be in real trouble for bringing other people on business. "I don't think they're following us," he tried to bluff.

"Let's find out. Make the next right." It was 112th Street in Manhattan. I had him make the standard four rights in succession. The Chevy stayed right behind us. "I told you, those fuckers are after me," I said as convincingly as I could.

"Son of a bitch," he said almost as believably.

"Okay, let's lose 'em," I cheered.

He didn't seem to want to do that. "How?"

"Like this." Without a warning I leaned across and jammed my left foot down on top of his right foot, sending the accelerator to the floorboard. The car jerked forward and then took off.

"TAKE YOUR FOOT OFF. TAKE YOUR FOOT OFF!" I took my foot off. We were going about 50 down the street when I moved back. Squillante understood what I had in mind. He also understood that I wasn't kidding around. He made a few quick turns, made a few yellow lights, and lost the Chevy, someplace in the wilds of Spanish Harlem.

We were alone.

The silence got louder and louder as we drove toward the bridge. "What are you gonna do to this guy when I point him out?" he broke in.

I shrugged my shoulders. "Nothin' tonight. I just want to know who he is."

"I'll tell you why, 'cause if you're gonna burn him, I don't want any part of it. I'm not a getaway driver, I'm a controller."

I reassured him. "Don't worry, Joe, you won't be driving any getaway car tonight." I paused. "And what makes you think I do heavyweight work?"

He kind of edged his head from side to side. "Well, you know, the word around the neighborhood was, you know, that you did. And things I hear from people now and then, you know, you got a reputation. I mean, like, I don't really know, but I *know*."

I chuckled. What he knew was going to hurt him. "Yeah, I guess so. The word gets around, doesn't it?"

He agreed that it did.

"Then how come you didn't fire when you saw it was me? I mean, how did you know I wasn't sent by whoever you pissed off?"

"I didn't. I just took a chance." Bullshit. He chickened out. "I just couldn't pull the trigger when I saw it was you." That I believed.

As we drove over the 59th Street Bridge, the Queensboro Bridge officially, I wondered what was going on in his mind. Did he know? Did he suspect? I stared at his head and picked out one small spot, just behind his right ear, that I would fire at. Normally I don't like to be this close to my target, three feet is usually plenty close enough and I was less than two feet away. In fact, if I reached my arm out, I would be at point blank range. I didn't want his head to explode all over me, that would make getting away clean a little more difficult.

I reached my hand into my jacket and checked to see that the silencer was still attached tightly to the gun. It was. Squillante was babbling on about the old neighborhood. I should have killed him just for being boring.

" . . . gamble," he said. I wasn't paying attention, so I only caught the last word. "Do you?"

"What?" I asked.

"Lose a lot when you gamble? Get way behind?"

"I can't afford it. Make this right here," I said, and then I told him exactly where we were going. I named the restaurant. "You ever been there?"

He said he hadn't.

"You should try it someday," I told him. "It's a whole meal for one price. All you can eat. And the food is pretty decent. You should take the old lady there one day."

"I will." We both were lying. I knew he wasn't going to live long enough ever to go there. He thought he would be leaving for Europe two days from now.

I really couldn't imagine him in Europe. When mob people run they almost always stay in the country. Very few leave these hospitable shores. I doubted if he would make it over there even if he had lived to get

222

away. I laughed inside. Here I was sitting next to this guy who was breathing, who was alive, and already I was thinking of him in the past tense.

The last hour had been a tough one for a man in my profession. I like things orderly and absolutely nothing had gone right. And worst of all, I had lost the killing emotion, I was relaxing. Now, as we got closer to the restaurant, I started letting it build up inside me, just staring at Squillante.

"You know, I was thinking that . . ." he started to say.

I stared right at him. "Not now, huh? Just shut it for awhile."

He looked at me and then looked straight ahead. I think that at that moment, for one brief second, just an instant in time, he knew. Then he denied it to himself.

We reached the restaurant just past midnight. "Pull way in the back of the lot," I told him. He drove to the rear and started pulling in next to another car. "Not here," I ordered. "Move it over there, in that dark spot. I don't want anyone to know we're here."

He started to protest. "Nobody knows this car."

"Just do it, huh? That's what you're being paid for right? To listen to me? So listen to me."

As he moved into the parking spot I reached into my jacket and got a good solid grip on the new .38. I was looking around the parking lot quickly, my instincts once again sharp, trying to spot someone, anyone, who might be a potential witness. One car was just pulling out of the place, all the way on the other side of the lot. No way they could spot anything. The lot itself was well lit, but the spot we moved into was shaded and dark.

I kept the gun inside my jacket until he had stopped

the car, put it in park, turned the engine off, turned the lights off, and then turned to face me. Then I took it out and pointed it right at him. He saw the gun and froze. I mean froze solid.

Panic strikes people in different ways. Some individuals immediately understand the situation, realize the hopelessness, and accept it as the final irony. Others start to scream. Some try but nothing comes out. From Squillante I got fear. In the one split second before I started to pump bullets into his head he crunched his body up, leaned hard against the door, and stuck both his hands out toward me as if in an effort to ward off the bullets. He knew. At the last second he knew.

"So long, Joe," I said in that brief moment. I don't know why I said anything. I can't remember ever saying anything on a job before, but I can distinctly remember myself saying, "so long, Joe," to him. It was the only sound before the shots and the words sounded tremendously loud.

Then I started firing into his head. The spot I had selected was turned away from me when he cringed, so I just fired randomly into his skull. The .38 made a muffled "pop" as I fired, the silencer almost completely covering the gunshots. No one standing outside the car could have heard anything.

The force of the first bullet drove his head to the left and against the window. The second bullet and the third bullet made his body jerk, but I'm quite sure he was dead when the first bullet smashed into his brain. All three hit their mark because, at that distance, it would have been impossible to miss.

There was no great spurt of blood all over the place, but a hard, steady stream flowed down the front of his face, running alongside his nose and then veering off to the side of his mouth.

After I stopped firing the momentum of the bullets made his body slump down, straight down, then against his door. For a slight moment I thought he was going to hit the horn, which was something I neither needed nor wanted, but he missed the steering wheel completely.

I sat in the car and unscrewed the silencer. I put it in one pocket and the fired .38 in the other.

Before getting out of the car I made sure Squillante's body was lying low enough so that no one who wasn't standing right next to the car could see it. Then I turned around to see if there was anybody in the parking lot. There was a group of four people walking into the restaurant. I sat there and watched as they disappeared inside the rear entrance. Then I got out of the car and, staying in the rear of the lot, keeping to the shadows, I walked away.

I never looked back.

AFTER THE BALL
IS OVER

Getting the job done was only half the fun. Even a well-executed hit is going to bring little satisfaction if you get caught before getting rid of the evidence: in this case, the new .38 and the silencer.

There are some people who do not pay too much attention to getting rid of the piece they work with. They heave it in the woods or throw it in the water or hide it behind their underwear in their top drawer. In the trade we have a word to describe people who do things like that: convicts. Guns have a way of coming back to haunt you. Not too many people know it, but the New York City Police Department has a special squad of skin divers that do nothing but look for things like guns. I can assure them they will never find one with my fingerprints on it.

I know that the only thing that can connect me to Squillante is the .38-with-silencer I have tucked in my jacket pocket. I'm not going to get rid of it simply and risk some kid accidentally finding it, I'm going to destroy it completely and for good. Once the job itself is done, that is my primary objective.

As soon as Squillante slumped over on the front seat I stopped thinking about him. He was finished as far as both of us were concerned. I walked out of the parking lot, trying to figure a way to get back to Manhattan and my own car. I wasn't worried about the car I left back at Bronx Park. There was nothing in it to connect it with me. I was going to drop it anyway, now I would just leave it there. Let the police find it.

As I walked I did my best to check my clothing out in the bad light. I wanted to make sure I hadn't ended up with any of his blood on me. I hadn't.

My problem was getting back to New York City without meeting anybody. I certainly couldn't hitch, I didn't want anybody picking me up anywhere near the parking lot. And I didn't want to grab a cab in the middle of nowhere. Most cabbies will remember if they pick somebody up walking along the road late at night, and I didn't want anyone remembering me. So I walked toward lights. I really didn't know the neighborhood too well, but I figured if I could find an open bar I could call a cab and the driver wouldn't think anything about it. My first choice would have been the subway to Manhattan, but I was a long way from any subway station.

I walked about 20 minutes. The whole trip I was thinking how this was just another foul-up in what had been the worst hit I ever made. And then, just to top everything off wonderfully well, it started raining again.

I found my bar and I sat down and had a quick beer before doing anything. Then I called a local cab company that had its name pasted on the phone and ordered a taxi. It arrived about ten minutes and a second beer later.

I took this cab into mid-Manhattan, then I grabbed

a second cab back up to the all-night garage in the Bronx. Finally, almost an hour and a half after burning Squillante, I got into my own car. All I wanted to do was get rid of the weapon, as far as I was concerned I had been holding it too long already. The first thing I did after pulling out of the garage was turn the radio on. Music calms the savage beast—and it also relaxes the hell out of a hit man. I headed back down into Manhattan, toward the lower tip, the Battery. I had very specific plans on how I was going to get rid of the gun and silencer.

I took the East River Drive downtown because I was pretty sure I wouldn't have to fight traffic at that hour. I tend to get uptight and angry when I'm caught in a traffic jam, and uptight and angry was something I didn't want to be. On the way down I reviewed the job once again. It wasn't the smoothest in the history of the world, but it was done. I wondered if Jackie was still struggling to get his hands free. I doubted it very much. I knew my treatment was not going to increase his great love for me, but there really wasn't very much else I could do under the circumstances. I figured I might hear some nasty words from the Fat Man, but business, as they say, is business.

By the time I reached the Battery it was almost two-thirty in the morning. New York City is really a beautiful place at that hour, especially after it's been raining for awhile. All the grime and dirt is hidden by the dark or washed away and the lights from the buildings reflect on the water. It really is an ideal, mystic time, a time for romantic people, of which I am not one.

I figured with good luck Squillante's body would not be discovered until the next morning. With bad luck somebody leaving the restaurant had to take a piss and went near the car and found what was left. I figured as long as I got rid of everything before Sunday noon I would have no problems. I knew there was a slim chance I would be hustled by the cops. Every time there's a gang hit they round up some "knowns," so the papers can make it look like they are doing something.

I parked my car in the lot right near the ferry landing and waited to board the boat to Staten Island. I wasn't nervous or upset at all. Also, interestingly enough, I wasn't the slightest bit cold, even though it was much colder down by the water than it had been in the Bronx. In fact, I felt one long bead of sweat wind its way slowly down my spine.

The ferry left for Staten Island on the hour. Most of the people on the boat were kids, couples taking a traditional Saturday night ride on the ferry. There was one couple in particular I didn't understand. A real faggy looking guy, skinny, long hair, bell-bottomed trousers, rings on almost all his fingers, and he was with this super-beautiful chick. This broad had a body that would stop a war. I couldn't understand what a looker like that was doing with a skinny nothing like him. Little did I know then, in 1968, that the fag look was going to get so popular. I stared but I didn't really care, to each his own.

I stood by myself near the railing. Nobody paid the slightest attention to me. When we were halfway to the Island dock I reached into my pocket and pulled out the silencer. Plunk! I dropped it casually into the river and watched as it sunk right to the bottom. If the million-to-one shot hits and the police find the silencer, what do they have? A rusty silencer and no gun to connect it with.

Why did I bother to throw the silencer away after

spending good money for it? I just don't want the thing to be found around me after I've used it. Especially after the law discovers somebody got hit in the parking lot of a busy restaurant, and since nobody heard the shots, they got to figure they're looking for a silencer. It's really just another safety precaution for my own piece of mind. I knew the currents would eventually pick it up and deposit it far away. The gun, which is a lot heavier, would have laid there longer. I held onto it. I had plans for it.

I got off the ferry for a minute and then got right back on. At that hour there are a lot of people who do exactly that, people just out for a boatride, so nobody pays any attention. Under normal conditions five minutes on Staten Island is too long, and these were certainly not normal circumstances. When we docked at the Battery, I picked up my car and headed back to the Bronx.

My exact destination was the South Bronx. A friend of mine has a small machine shop to which I hold one key, to be used on just such occasions as this. The place wasn't big, but it was spooky quiet. I get more nervous in places like this than I do before gunning an individual. The quiet bothers me. I like noise, I like people, I like things happening. In this case, all I wanted to do was finish my work as quickly as possible.

The only light I put on in the place was the fluorescent lamp he had over his workbench. From the outside no one could tell it wasn't an interior light left on all night to scare away burglars.

The first thing I went to work on was the barrel. I grabbed an electrical hack saw and cut it right off at the base. Then I cut it in two pieces the long way, down the seam. Next, I took each of those pieces and cut them in half, lengthwise again. Now what was once the barrel was just four long pieces of metal.

Then I went after the hammer. I was right at home with these tools. I always had the ability to work with my hands and make nice things in the shop. The few times I've seriously thought about retirement I always end up looking for something to do with tools.

I propped the piece up on the workbench, opened the hammer and then smashed the shit out of it with a heavy hand hammer. There was absolutely no way that gun was going to come back to haunt me. I smashed the firing pin because, even if the coppers come up with the cartridges, without a firing pin there is absolutely no way they can match it up to a gun. I finally had the whole thing dismantled.

I took all the pieces and put them in a paper bag. I got back in my car and started touring the Bronx, looking for sewers. Looking for sewers in the Bronx at 2 A.M. Sunday morning is not my favorite occupation in the world, so I tried to make it brief. Every time I found another sewer, I would carefully wipe all fingerprints off one individual piece and deposit that piece into the sewer for posterity. I threw the cylinder in one place. The stock went in another. Then each part of the barrel. There simply ain't no one in the world who could find all those pieces and put them back together.

This all sounds like a lot of trouble and it is. But after making a hit, especially one with all the problems that this one had, you are all keyed up anyway and you really need something to do to keep busy. Some men are able to go out and eat dinner, some guys get laid. Me? I take my time getting rid of the weapon. Then, if it can be arranged, I go out for dinner and get laid.

The whole disposal operation, from the moment

Squillante died until I finished spreading the gun, took about four hours. It was getting to be toward morning when I finally finished my labors. Now I could go home and try to get some sleep. Sunday was supposed to be a work day. My cigarettes were arriving and I planned to be at the warehouse.

I really felt tired when I laid down, but I just could not get to sleep. My wife was dead to the world when I got home and, as promised, I didn't wake her, but I couldn't get to sleep myself. Normally I have no problem putting my head on the pillow and zonking out, but I guess the tension of the night was taking its time unwinding.

About 6 A.M. I really made a second effort. I remember tossing and turning for awhile and then I guess I drifted off in a semisleep. I did not dream about Joseph Squillante. This ain't the movies.

My old lady woke me just after noon. She did it simply by getting out of bed herself, I wasn't sleeping very soundly. I opened one eye and kind of mumbled, "Everything go okay last night?" No answer. She was obviously upset. "Everything go okay last night I said," I repeated.

"Everything was alright last night," was the answer I got, she didn't even look at me.

I was trying to get a conversation going. If I can do that I can usually make her forget whatever she's mad about. "Anybody call?"

She really didn't want to answer, but she did. "Nobody called." She stopped for a moment, "I want you to call your brother today and apologize."

"That's a good idea." I was going to agree with whatever she said. If she said she wanted me to fuck myself I would have said "that's a good idea." She still hadn't looked at me. Based on her replies, I knew she was not going to be thrilled if I asked her to make breakfast. In this case cowardice overcame hunger and I didn't dare ask. I figured I'd pick something up on the way to the warehouse.

"Did your *business* work out alright last night?" This was her way of asking a sarcastic question.

"Yeah, fine," I told her honestly. "Perfect." It was the first time since waking up that I thought about Squillante. In that short period of time I had literally put him out of my mind. I had closed his case permanently.

She mumbled something else but I really didn't pay too much attention. Slowly, and not without some trouble, I rolled over and sat up. I was really tired. I had something like a hangover. Somehow I managed to get into the bathroom and throw some cold water on my face. One at a time, very uneasily, my eyes opened. They were not happy to see so much light so early in the day. The first thing I did, once my heart started beating regularly, was to try to call my brother. His line was busy so I called Bobby Roach. Next to my brother, money is the thing closest to my heart. "What's the story?" I asked him.

"Nothing yet," he said in his best professional tone. "The trucks should be here by four. I'm going to watch the first pro game and then go over."

"You got some kids coming over to break up the cartons?" Taking the cartons of cigarettes out of the boxes and filling orders is probably the biggest pain-in-the-ass job in cigarette bootlegging. The job itself can take almost a full day when you've got 40,000 cartons and 20 or 30 orders to fill. We usually hire some local kids and give them five bucks an hour, plus a good tip when the job is done, just to help them keep their heads on straight. I consider it a community service—it keeps the kids off the streets.

"You comin' over?" the Roach asked me.

"I'm gonna try," I said. "I'm gonna watch the game, but if it gets out of hand I'll come over early."

"You can come early anyways," he offered. "I got one of those small portable Sony's off a truck a few weeks ago and I'll bring that along. It'll make the work go easier."

Inside, I sighed. The old crime business sure has gotten soft.

I made the first section of the Four Star *Sunday News* final. I found out about an hour after I spoke to the Roach. Since my brother's line was still busy I decided to go out for breakfast and pick up the Four Star along the way.

I don't collect press clippings, scrapbooks are not healthy things to keep around the house, but I do need to know what everybody else knows about my business. I didn't bother to get the *Times,* the *News* is the paper for murders, the *Times* for wars, a well-known fact. The story was buried—that's a newspaper term, not a hit man's—about ten pages deep. It was obvious they didn't have very much information. The story basically said that a body had been found in the front seat of a late-model car by the cook as he was leaving the restaurant about 5 A.M. The thus-far unidentified driver had been shot three times in the head in "gangland fashion." The story went on to say that the police were investigating. Which meant they didn't have anything.

The average New York City detective is underpaid and overworked. He has more murders on his hands than he can handle, and he's going to get the same paycheck every week whether he solves them or not.

So he's going to be selective in choosing the cases he actually puts time on. Honest-citizen n.urders are going to get the bulk of his time. Chances are a gangland rubout will not be high on his list of selections. It's really a who-gives-a-damn case. There's little glory and a lot of hassles involved. Besides, even if there was enough manpower, there is still a shortage in thinking. There are not many Colombos or Ironsides on the NYPD. Without an informant, an eyewitness or a gun, their chances of figuring out what the case is all about are almost nonexistent. Therefore, once I leave the scene of a crime I'm usually pretty safe.

Usually.

I don't know how they found me, or why they bothered, but they picked me up Monday afternoon as I was coming out of Aqueduct. Sunday had been a productive day. My football picks were pretty good and we filled the cigarette orders. The deliveries started on Monday and I wasn't needed at the warehouse until the evening to pick up the cash, so I celebrated by rushing around to see my bookmaking customers and dashing out to the track.

I was walking toward my car when these two individuals walked up to me and asked, "Are you Joseph so-and-so?"

I made them as detectives right away. The cut of their cloth. Basic Robert Hall. "You know I am," I said, "or you wouldn't have asked."

They both smiled. We all knew the routine. I wasn't surprised at the fact that they had come around to see me, what did surprise me is that they bothered to track me all the way to Aqueduct, and then stand waiting by my car, rather than simply coming by my apartment and picking me up. As I've said, after every hit the coppers will pick up some people just to show they are on the job. They really don't have any idea who did the deed, no leads, no clues, but the chief says make a sweep, so they make a sweep.

"Want to put up your hands?" Physically they were both big men, much taller than me and, as usual, very polite. I've found that detectives very rarely get nasty. They just do their jobs according to rules and regulations, and nobody gets hurt. I didn't mind them searching me because I knew they weren't going to find anything. After I make a hit I never, never carry a gun on me or in my car for a few days. I do very little except relax. In fact, if I read about a hit in the *News* that I think I might get picked up for, I stop carrying a gun. Better safe than sorry. I know that if I have to get my hands on a gun I can get one pretty damn quick.

I put my hands straight up in the air and held them rigid, an exaggerated jumping jack. "Like this?"

"Something like that," one of them said. "Would you lean against the car please?"

I pushed my weight forward and did as asked. As I did I thought of Sweetlips doing precisely the same thing Saturday night. It seemed like years ago. I stood against the car and one of the detectives ran down my body. He wasn't dumb enough to expect to find anything. Finally he asked, "You mind if we search your car?"

I did my usual number. "You guys got a search warrant?"

They looked at each other. Obviously they didn't. I shrugged my shoulders. "Go ahead, boys, make yourselves happy. Search the car." I know there's nothing in there, so why not. By this time that car is so clean it would warm the heart of a car-wash attendant, so let them search to their hearts' content. I handed the keys to the detective standing nearest the door and he opened up and started feeling around. By this time we were starting to draw a crowd in the parking lot and that I did not particularly appreciate. "Listen," I said to the guy standing next to me, "is this a pinch?"

"Not really. We just want to ask you some questions."

"So ask."

The second detective finished his search. "Nothing," he said to his partner. Then he turned to me. "We were told to bring you in."

I could see this was going to be a pain in the behind. "What the fuck do we have to bother with that for?" I asked them. "Just go ahead and ask your fucking questions."

"Not here," the same individual said with some force. "You've got to come in with us. We can do it the easy way or the hard way."

This was fascinating. I was hearing my own words thrown back at me. I've used that same warning phrase at least 50 times. And since I know the inevitable outcome, I also know the best choice.

"My chariot awaits," I shrugged and we went the easy way. I drove with one of them alongside me and his partner drove their car in. We headed toward their headquarters. I hope all of this made the late not-so-great Joe Squillante happy.

COPPING OUT

My partner for the ride identified himself as Detective Maurice Braverman, NYPD. Maurice seemed to be in his mid-30s, over six feet and showed the beginnings of what would assuredly become a pot belly, an occupational hazard on the detective force. He didn't seem to want to be in my car any more than I wanted him there. I think both of us realized this was a complete waste of time. At least I hoped he did.

"Where we going?" I asked.

When these boys identified themselves they neglected to tell me what borough they were from. This is an old device. I was simply supposed to drive to the borough the crime was committed in without any direction. And when I do that the coppers know that I know exactly what crime they're interested in. New York City cops are not dopes. If you slip, they're going to catch you before you hit the ground. Some of them may be crooks, some of them may be on the take (although homicide cops certainly aren't), but they know their jobs.

There wasn't too much conversation in the car. At one point I asked if he had any idea what this was all about. He avoided the question as a good copper always does, "You'll find out when you get there."

Later he asked me, "How'd you do with the animals?"

I had won some bucks, but I didn't see any reason to share this information.

"Why?" I asked. "You want to become my partner?" He laughed. I could see he was just as bored as I was.

"Let's follow Kenny," Maurice told me. Kenny was Detective Kenneth Willins, his partner. We went right to the precinct house not far from the track, in the heart of Queens. I understood why they picked me up at the track: convenience. What I didn't know was how they knew I was there. I asked.

Maurice shrugged his shoulders. "A friend of yours told us we might find you out there."

"I don't have any friends," I said, still trying to find out who they spoke to.

He thought about that for a minute. "Maybe you don't," he finally agreed.

We went directly into a small, empty conference room with the usual long table and four holding chairs. There was absolutely nothing on the wall except a little peeling paint. The room was a lot like those interrogation rooms you see in old movies, except it was lit by a long fluorescent light rather than a single uncovered light bulb. Maurice offered me a chair and suggested I sit and wait. I obliged him.

Then another individual came into the room. He didn't identify himself, but I assumed he was the resident assistant district attorney. I was not particularly thrilled to see him. Normally in roundups they just bring you in, have the coppers question you, then let you go. The ADAs don't get involved unless there's hope for making a real case.

The first thing he did was read my rights to me. I heard them so often I know them better than the pledge of allegiance. I had the right to an attorney. I didn't have to answer any questions. Wonderful, I told them, I'm not going to answer any questions and I want my attorney present. (This is much better than the old days when your rights consisted of being beaten up in the back room of the stationhouse.)

"If you're not guilty," the ADA asked, "what do you want an attorney for?"

It was a legitimate question and I had a legitimate answer for it. "None of your fucking business," I told him. "You guys got degrees, I don't. You guys being so smart, you're going to ask me tough questions and me being so stupid, I'm liable to give you the wrong answers. My attorney will tell me what I answer and what I don't answer."

Maurice came forward and said something to this guy. The guy backed off. Old Maurice obviously was going to be my friend. He played the role perfectly, beginning by offering me a cigarette. "Hey, just relax a minute, okay?" he said as he perched himself on the table.

I had all the friends I needed. "No fucking way, pal. Either I walk out of here right now or my lawyer comes down. If you think you got me for anything, go ahead and book me."

Maurice looked back at the other guy for direction. The ADA nodded. Finally, Maurice, no longer my best friend, said, "Okay, go ahead and call your lawyer."

That threw me back. I smiled on the outside but inside I did not feel so terribly wonderful. The only reason I pushed the lawyer issue was I didn't feel like sitting around in this room all afternoon. I had customers to see. And, normally, when I pushed the issue, they would let me take a walk. They'll only go through the lawyer hassle if they really think they have something. So I called my lawyer, quickly.

I didn't care if this convinced them I had something to hide or not, because I knew one thing they couldn't possibly know. I knew I was guilty. I wanted a lawyer there from the very beginning, another security precaution.

I've used a number of different attorneys in my career. I judge them by only one thing: How quickly they can walk me out the door. I don't want to know about fees (it's the responsibility of the guys who hired me to take care of my legal expenses), I don't want to know about problems and pleadings. I want to know how soon I'm going to get out.

My attorney at this point was, and still is in fact, a good Jewish hustler. Aaron Goldberg, as we shall call my attorney, walked me out the door. Goldberg is a smallish man with glasses and a receding hairline. You can see a hundred Aaron Goldbergs outside any United Jewish Appeal rally, but this was the original. He had started doing low-income work for poor people, got a few rich clients, bought into some buildings, found out his real-estate ventures had some partners within the organization, let them show him how he could increase the value of his investments, defended a few of them on a variety of charges and won. And now he's a very wealthy, somewhat powerful individual. He was recommended to me by a former lawyer, an individual who made the mistake of suggesting we agree to accept a manslaughter charge instead of first-degree murder.

When I called him this time he got down to the stationhouse just as fast as his Mercedes could carry him. I am not one of Aaron's best clients. He doesn't make a lot of money off me. What he does make is points with the organization. And eventually a smart man like Aaron Goldberg will turn those points into dollars. While we were waiting, the coppers tried to ask me a few questions, but I kept my trap shut. I didn't care what they thought, what they thought didn't matter. It was what they could prove that caused the problems.

I quickly went over the job step by step. I could not figure out any mistakes. If I had a problem I took a guess that I was seen by someone who shouldn't have seen me. That had happened before. Twice. One time the witnesses decided to go on vacation before my trial came up and I was released when they didn't show. The second time the potential witness realized he had made a mistake and I was not the guilty party. That realization saved all of our lives.

As soon as Goldberg got there he started making a lovely fuss. He started screaming that his client had been illegally detained (I hadn't been) and demanded that I be immediately released. That was his game and, of course, it didn't work. Finally he calmed down and asked to be left alone in the room with his client. Me. Everybody else left.

The two most important rules I've learned to live with are: Take good care of your wife and never lie to your lawyer. I knew I could tell Goldberg everything because an attorney-client conversation is privileged, meaning no part of it can ever be used against the client. Also, I knew the coppers were not stupid enough to have the room wired because it would most probably cause every case in the precinct to be thrown out of court.

Goldberg looked at me with that mournful look more normal on sheepdogs. It was obvious he didn't want to be here. "Okay," he sighed, "let's have it. What do they think they have?" Up until this point it never occurred to me that Goldberg didn't have the slightest idea what this case was about. I had assumed someone had told him. Then I realized the cops had never mentioned it to me either.

"Murder."

He shook his head. This time he didn't even look at me. I think he knew the answer before he asked the question. "Did you?"

I nodded.

He shook his head once again in disbelief and gave a fake chuckle. "What do you have to do these things for? Why can't you get into something safe like dope smuggling?" He took off his glasses and wiped them. "What happened?"

I told him the whole story. I told him about Squillante. I told him why he went. I told him about getting picked up by the coppers. I told him how I pulled this job. The only thing I didn't tell him were the names of the people who contacted me and hired me. Now Goldberg knows enough about the case to turn me every way but loose. And then we went through the whole thing again.

"Okay," he said after hearing it a second time, "is it possible they have anything at all?"

"Anything is possible."

"Witnesses?"

"I didn't see any." I paused and thought about Jackie Sweetlips. Inside I laughed. His way of getting even? An anonymous telephone tip? It wasn't his style, but it was possible. And he was a witness to our departure, at least. But he couldn't get me involved because he was involved. If I went, and I found out he had set me up, he was going to go too.

And what about the two punks? The hold-up men. How about them? I just didn't think so. In the dark, at the distance they were sitting, there was no way they could positively identify me even if they knew who I was, which they didn't. They could find out. They had my license-plate number. But they weren't about to go to the police. I remembered Sweetlips on the floor, talking for his life, "Joey, those punks got nothin' to gain and their lives to lose if they turn you in."

"Where's the gun?"

"I destroyed it."

"Are you sure the guy died?"

"Does the *Daily News* lie?" We both laughed.

He reached into his briefcase and took out a legal pad. "Here's what I want you to do," he said. "When they come back in and start asking questions, answer them as best you can. I'll tell you when to stop when you're going too far. I want to find out if they really have anything. And Joey, listen to me. When I tell you to shut up, you shut up."

"You're the doctor," I agreed.

"Believe me," he said, "it would have been easier than being your lawyer."

I told Goldberg one more thing. So far the coppers had not mentioned why they brought me down. I didn't want him giving away the fact that we already were aware of the problem.

We invited the coppers back into the room. I was beginning to look at my watch because I still had hopes of getting to the garage that night, as well as seeing some customers. It was already almost six o'clock.

"My client and I agreed he should answer some of your questions," Goldberg told them. "I'll tell him when to stop. Let me just begin by telling you my client has no idea why he is here. He has advised me he has done nothing wrong."

The assistant district attorney started the questioning. "Do you know . . ."

Goldberg interrupted. "I'm sorry, I didn't get your name."

The ADA looked at him. "Steven Boswell," he said, "I'm in the district attorney's office."

Goldberg stuck out his hand. "Aaron Goldberg. Nice to meet you."

"Yeah," ADA Boswell agreed, "nice to make your acquaintance." He turned back to me. "Do you know Joseph Squillante?"

"Which Joseph Squillante? There's ten thousand of them in New York. That's a pretty common name."

"He lived up on Roberts Avenue."

I thought carefully for a moment. "I don't believe I know the gentleman. I don't know anybody who lives up there."

"He originally came from your neighborhood."

Instant recognition. "Oh yeah, I knew one Joseph Squillante," I said, putting the emphasis on "one." "He runs numbers in the Bronx. I grew up with him. And, and you're not going to believe this, but my old lady and me bumped into him and his old lady at Macy's about two weeks ago. Is that the guy?"

Boswell nodded.

"What about him?" I asked.

"He was found dead yesterday. Shot in the head three times."

"Oh?" I asked with as much surprise as I could muster.

"Didn't you read the papers?"

"Only the race results. I don't worry about what's on the front end. It don't bother me." I looked at Goldberg for some direction, but he was making notes on his yellow legal paper. While I was answering these questions, I tried to figure out what the coppers had in mind. I wasn't worried, but I was concerned. I've played this question-and-answer game too many times to enjoy it. And once it ended up with me spending almost a year in the House of Detention, the Tombs, in New York City waiting to be tried. (And waiting for the witnesses to plan their vacation.) The thought that I might end up there again did not fill me with great happiness. I asked for some water.

Maurice, who had been standing quietly in the background, left to get the water. The line of questioning changed. "How much money do you have with you?"

"Right now?"

"Right now."

"I don't know," I said, and I didn't. I made a guess. "Six, seven hundred maybe."

"Where do you get your money?"

"I don't thin . . ." I started to say in an angry voice.

"What my client is about to say," Goldberg interrupted, "is that he would prefer not to answer that question."

"Is that right?" Boswell asked.

"Perfectly," I agreed with Goldberg.

"Okay," Boswell said, "don't answer." Maurice returned with my water. As I started sipping it the questioning honed in. "What were you doing in Queens Saturday night around midnight?"

It was a good question. If I came up with an answer at all I would be admitting I was in the borough. "I wasn't," I told him, "I was home."

"Can you prove it?"

"I don't have to. I don't have to prove nothin'. You're the people who got to prove I did or I don't or I was or I wasn't."

Goldberg laughed.

"What kind of car do you drive?"

I told him.

"That's a nice car," he said.

"Yeah, I got a good deal on it."

There was a lot of moving and shifting around by everyone except Goldberg and myself. I just sat there, hands folded on the table, leaning back to stretch occasionally. Goldberg kept writing away.

"You own a gun?"

"ME?" I was somewhat astonished. Goldberg held a cautious finger up in the air. "Don't you know that would be against the law?" I asked. Goldberg put his finger down and returned to his writing.

It was right at this point that I began to think they really didn't have much of anything except a hunch. But why me? Sweetlips had to be the answer. Or maybe just a lucky guess on their part, it has happened to other people. But their questioning was so general that I figured they were trying to make a hopefa case— they were hoping for any kind of clue that would give me up.

For the first time since we were at Aqueduct, the other detective, Willins, opened his mouth. "You know you were spotted in Queens Saturday night?"

I raised my eyebrows. "That's interesting," I said calmly. This was possible, but I doubted it. And this is also the one thing you can depend on the cops telling you in this type of situation. They always tell you that you did something wrong, someone saw you, you left a print, the guy didn't die right away and identified you. Something. Unless the individual sitting on the hot seat is an idiot, he'll just ignore it. This isn't TV. "I think it must be a case of mistaken identity."

"We'll see," he said, "when we line you up."

Now there was some bad news. If they were going to have a lineup I might indeed have some problems. That means that somebody really did see something and the police think they can pin it down. And police have been known to rig a lineup, lining up five guys and one black giant when the witness knows a big nigger did the job. I was not thrilled to hear about the lineup at all, and I think my face must have given a little something away.

But Boswell and Maurice were so busy being intelligent with their own questions they didn't pick it up. "Will you take a paraffin test?" Boswell asked. This is a test that determines if you've fired a weapon recently. I wasn't sure what the test would show. It had been more than 36 hours since I killed Squillante, and I was wearing gloves at the time. But I wasn't about to agree to any sort of test at all.

"No," I said. "No way."

"Why not?"

"I don't feel like it. I don't have to. And I don't want to. That's three reasons." I stared right back at him. They can't even force you to be fingerprinted if you don't want to, much less take a paraffin test. It happens to be against your legal rights for them to force you to give up your fingerprints without your consent, until you've been convicted, of course. But when they bring you in, they can't fingerprint you.

There is one catch. They do have the right to hold

you until they can identify you to their satisfaction. That could be 30 years or at least a pain-in-the-neck. It's much easier to give them your prints. When you're released you can demand they destroy your records anyway.

I was getting a little tired of this whole thing at about this point. Joe Squillante was simply not worth all this trouble. "Are you guys going to be much longer?" I asked.

Boswell laughed. "That depends on you." And then we went through the entire routine designed to trap unwary hit men.

Question: Do you know so-and-so from the Bronx?

Answer: Never heard of him.

Question: Where did Squillante come from?

Answer: My block in the Bronx.

Question: Have you ever eaten at this particular restaurant where the body was found?

Answer: The food there is terrible. You can die from food poisoning.

Question: Who were you with Saturday night?

Answer: My wife. Ask her.

Question: Did Squillante ever place a bet with any individuals you know?

Answer: I don't know any individuals that take bets.

Question: How much were you paid?

Answer: For what? What you talking about?

Statement: Why don't you tell us about it? This time we have a witness.

Statement: Fuck off and fuck your witness. I was home with my wife.

This went on for about an hour, with the questions always coming back to Squillante. The police'll batter

you with questions up one side and down the other if
you allow them to.

Finally Goldberg decided enough was enough. "Do
you gentlemen have any further questions for my
client?"

Boswell looked at Maurice. "Why don't we set the
lineup up now?" I looked at Goldberg and raised my
eyebrows. He smiled. Maurice left the room. "You
know," Boswell said casually to me, "if you tell us
about it now, we'll make it a lot easier for you. I
think we can probably get it down to manslaughter.
But you have to do it now. After we make our case
we're gonna follow through on it." He waited.
"Whattya say."

"Kiss my ass."

He shrugged his shoulders. "It's your funeral." Five
minutes passed. Ten. Twenty. And then, then it came
to me. The witness. There was only one person it
could possibly be. Nice Mrs. Gibson, the lady with the
Great Dane, had come back to haunt me. I snapped
my fingers as I realized it, drawing everyone's attention.

"Whatsamatta?" Boswell asked.

"My client had to snap his fingers," Goldberg said
before I could get a word out. "There's no law against
that yet, is there?"

"Not yet," Boswell agreed, "but give us time."

Good old, nice, warm, wonderful Mrs. Gibson,
everybody's grandmother, was about to fuck me. She
could cause lots and lots of problems, especially when
we went to trial. But she couldn't put me near the
murder scene or even connect me with Squillante. And
I could imagine what the jury would think after they
heard about Mrs. Gibson scouring her neighborhood
for a Great Dane that the prosecution would prove

never existed. That social-security collecting biddy was throwing me to the dogs.

I figured I'd better tell Goldberg. I leaned over and started whispering in his ear. "Actually," I started, "there was one thing I forgot to tell ya. You see, there was this little old lady . . ." I stopped as Maurice reentered. He whispered something in Boswell's ear and then left again. I stopped talking to Goldberg and waited for Boswell to say something.

"Last chance," Boswell said nicely.

Was she standing out there in the hall? Why not? I was the idiot who had told her to go to the police! Would she still be attached to that monster on the leash? I couldn't picture them any way but together.

Then, by an effort of will, I blanked her out. I killed her and her goddamn dog.

"Thanks, but no thanks," I said.

He took a deep breath. "Okay, the witness had to leave so we can't line you up now and we're not going to hold you. But stay around because we'll see you again as soon as we get her back."

Outside I laughed heavily. There was no witness. It was a trick, a clever trick, to talk me into confessing. I loved it. Boswell looked at Willins when I started laughing. I really think they believed I did it. They didn't have any evidence, or proof, but they believed I was guilty. They were obviously frustrated by the fact they couldn't do a damn thing about it.

Goldberg and I walked out of the stationhouse together. "You have any idea how they got onto you?"

"One," I said, thinking about Sweetlips, and realizing I wasn't going to do a damn thing about it. There would eventually be some sort of confrontation, but not over this. And I couldn't even be sure it was him. Still . . .

"Thank you, lawyer," I said to Goldberg. "Send me your bill and I'll have it taken care of."

"You want to get a cup of coffee?"

I checked my watch. It was past nine o'clock. "I can't. I gotta meet some people."

"That's okay. Call me when you need me."

"Don't worry," I told him, "I most certainly will."

I started to walk away but Goldberg stopped me. "One more thing," he asked, "what about that little old lady you started to tell me about?"

I laughed. "You would never believe it." I continued walking over to my car and started figuring what I had to do over the next few days. Number one, the cash from the cigarettes and meeting with Joe Cheese. Number two, my bookmaking customers on Tuesday. Beyond that I had no plans. I knew something would turn up. It always does.

I had a feeling my friends in the blue uniforms would be keeping an eye on me for awhile so I would have to be careful. That in itself wasn't so terrible. I had money in my pocket and it would give me more time to spend with the animals and with Alice-with-the-big-tits. I was almost hoping the coppers would trail me. It would fill my heart with joy to know that somebody else was sitting in the cold while *I* was inside balling some chick, like I had to do with Squillante.

Squillante. I gave him a brief thought. I guessed the funeral would be on Tuesday. I had no intention of going, or even sending flowers. Why add insult to injury?

I got in my car and turned the radio on. That same damn loud blaring music was in full swing. I took one deep breath and looked back at the stationhouse. Maurice and Kenny, NYPD, were just coming down the steps. As my car was warming up, I sat and watched as they walked toward me. They stopped when they got there and Maurice leaned in. The game was over, we all knew it, and they seemed more relaxed, more at ease.

"Did you do it?" he asked.

I'll never know how he knew, but he knew. Probably just a hunch, but he knew. "Whattya think?" I asked him.

"I think you did it," he said flatly.

I smiled at him. "Your mother would be proud of you." Then I put the car in drive and left them standing on the sidewalk.

All of which is how one Joseph Squillante came to be dead.

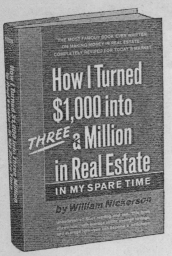